MAXnotes®

Ralph Waldo Ellison's

Invisible Man

Text by
David M. Gracer
(M.A., University of Wyoming)
Department of English
Mercy College
Dobbs Ferry, New York

Illustrations by
Bob Rodefeld

 *Research & Education Association*

MAXnotes® for
INVISIBLE MAN

Copyright © 1996 by Research & Education Association. All rights reserved. No part of this book may be reproduced in any form without permission of the publisher.

Printed in the United States of America

Library of Congress Catalog Card Number 96-67424

International Standard Book Number 0-87891-021-2

MAXnotes® is a registered trademark of
Research & Education Association, Piscataway, New Jersey 08854

What **MAXnotes**® *Will Do for You*

This book is intended to help you absorb the essential contents and features of Ralph Ellison's *Invisible Man* and to help you gain a thorough understanding of the work. The book has been designed to do this more quickly and effectively than any other study guide.

For best results, this **MAXnotes** book should be used as a companion to the actual work, not instead of it. The interaction between the two will greatly benefit you.

To help you in your studies, this book presents the most up-to-date interpretations of every section of the actual work, followed by questions and fully explained answers that will enable you to analyze the material critically. The questions also will help you to test your understanding of the work and will prepare you for discussions and exams.

Meaningful illustrations are included to further enhance your understanding and enjoyment of the literary work. The illustrations are designed to place you into the mood and spirit of the work's settings.

The **MAXnotes** also include summaries, character lists, explanations of plot, and section-by-section analyses. A biography of the author and discussion of the work's historical context will help you put this literary piece into the proper perspective of what is taking place.

The use of this study guide will save you the hours of preparation time that would ordinarily be required to arrive at a complete grasp of this work of literature. You will be well prepared for classroom discussions, homework, and exams. The guidelines that are included for writing papers and reports on various topics will prepare you for any added work which may be assigned.

The **MAXnotes** will take your grades "to the max."

Dr. Max Fogiel
Program Director

Contents

Section One: *Introduction* 1
   The Life and Work of Ralph Ellison 1
   Historical Background 2
   Master List of Characters 3
   Summary of the Novel 5
   Estimated Reading Time 6

> **Each Chapter includes List of Characters, Summary, Analysis, Study Questions and Answers, and Suggested Essay Topics.**

Section Two: *Invisible Man* 7
   Prologue 7
   Chapter 1 10
   Chapter 2 15
   Chapter 3 19
   Chapter 4 23

Chapter 5 26
Chapter 6 29
Chapter 7 33
Chapter 8 37
Chapter 9 39
Chapter 10 43
Chapter 11 47
Chapter 12 51
Chapter 13 54
Chapter 14 59
Chapter 15 63
Chapter 16 66
Chapter 17 70
Chapter 18 74
Chapter 19 80
Chapter 20 83
Chapter 21 88
Chapter 22 92
Chapter 23 95
Chapter 24 100
Chapter 25 103
Epilogue 108

Section Three: *Sample Analytical Paper Topics* 112

Section Four: *Bibliography* 115

SECTION ONE

Introduction

The Life and Work of Ralph Waldo Ellison

Ralph Waldo Ellison was born on March 1, 1914, in Oklahoma City, Oklahoma. He died on April 16, 1994, in Harlem, New York. He was named after Ralph Waldo Emerson, a great nineteenth century writer. When Lewis Ellison thought of the future, he saw his son, the poet.

The narrator of *Invisible Man* shows an interest in Ralph Waldo Emerson. The young Ralph Ellison felt a burden attached to this great name, a pressure to become great himself, and it made him uncomfortable.

Ralph Ellison did not grow up in the Deep South, as his parents had, and this made an important difference in his life. Oklahoma was a new territory, offering a chance for a better life than in the former slave states, despite the Jim Crow laws that white settlers brought with them.

Ellison went to Douglass High School (named after Frederick Douglass), and then to Tuskegee Institute, a well-known historically black college in Alabama, in June 1933. He was unhappy at Tuskegee, and his impressions of that college are reflected in the narrator's experiences with Dr. Bledsoe in *Invisible Man*. Ellison never finished his degree. Instead, he left for New York in the spring of 1936. The great promise of Harlem was calling his name.

Once he arrived, Ellison took odd jobs and met the leading black artists and intellectuals of his day. The atmosphere was vibrant, and Ellison, whose artistic abilities included music, sculpture, writing, and photography, participated in what was later called the Harlem Renaissance. Soon, through the encouragement of black American writer Richard Wright, author of *Native Son*, Ellison was publishing book reviews and short stories.

Ellison worked on *Invisible Man* for five years. It was published in 1952 and won the National Book Award for fiction. Ellison's only novel, it established his literary reputation. He also published two collections of essays: *Shadow and Act* in 1964, and *Going into the Territory* in 1986.

Ellison died in Harlem, New York, which had been his home for 20 years, and which he immortalized in his masterpiece, *Invisible Man*.

Historical Background

The physical and emotional segregation of an earlier American society is a main subject of *Invisible Man*. It is considered a classic because of its writing, and also for its portrayal of the experiences of African-Americans. At the same time, as Ellison himself had frequently asserted before his death, the book goes beyond specific questions of race relations. It touches upon the dynamics of personal identity, and the ways and limits in which people can know each other.

Though no specific years are given in the novel, there are clues for the reader. The shell-shocked men at the Golden Day, a local tavern and halfway house, respond to the name of General Pershing, indicating that World War I is part of their pasts. There is no mention of World War II. There is frequent mention of black people who contributed to the American experience earlier in this century, such as Louis Armstrong, Paul Robeson, and Joe Louis, as well as ideas that affected blacks, like Jim Crow laws.

One of the central themes of the novel is the extent to which its black characters feel free to express themselves in what they are told is a "white man's world." Whether this has changed is a matter of discussion and debate by trained professionals, such as sociologists and psychologists, and by students and working people as well.

Invisible Man was published in 1952. Some of its scenes anticipate the civil rights protests that would alter this country in that decade and the next. The first six chapters take place in the Deep

South. Then, like many black Americans who left the South for more hospitable places, the narrator departs for New York City. At first, he finds it to be the better world that some have told him about, but his optimism is eventually shattered.

Master List of Characters

The Narrator—*tells the story of his life, but remains unnamed throughout the novel.*

Grandfather—*although not appearing in the novel, he is an important influence on the narrator because of the deathbed scene.*

Jackson—*a particularly sadistic member of the audience at the battle royal. He tries to attack the blindfolded boys, but is restrained from doing so.*

Tatlock—*the very large, mean boy that the narrator is forced to fight at the battle royal.*

Mr. Norton—*an important benefactor of the college that the narrator attends.*

The Founder—*an almost mythical man, who founded the college the narrator attends. He is no longer alive. A statue of him stands on the campus, and many different characters talk about him, but the reader never finds out his name or the race to which he belonged.*

Dr. Bledsoe—*president of the college the narrator attends.*

Jim Trueblood—*a poor farmer on the land adjacent to the college.*

The Vet—*the man who helps Mr. Norton at the Golden Day tavern, and in the process tells some deep truths about the narrator's situation. The narrator talks with him again, on the bus.*

Big Halley—*the bartender at the Golden Day.*

Supercargo—*the attendent at the Golden Day.*

Sylvester—*a mental patient and client at the Golden Day.*

Edna—*a prostitute at the Golden Day.*

The Reverend Homer A. Barbee—*the man who gives the address at the narrator's college.*

Crenshaw—*the man in charge of taking the vet from the Golden Day to St. Elizabeth's Hospital, a well-known mental institution in Washington, D.C.*

Mr. Emerson's son—*the man who shows the narrator the contents of a letter written by Dr. Bledsoe.*

Mr. Kimbro and Mr. MacDuffy—*the white men at the Liberty Paint Factory.*

Lucius Brockway—*the man in charge of the boilers at the Liberty Paint Factory.*

Mary—*the woman who finds the narrator on the street and gives him a home.*

Ras the Exhorter—*a powerful leader of a major protest movement in Harlem. There is much conflict between his ideology and that of the Brotherhood movement. Near the end of the novel, Ras changes his name from "Ras the Exhorter" to "Ras the Destroyer."*

Brother Jack—*The first member of "the Brotherhood," a movement that the narrator becomes involved in after his experience in public speaking.*

Emma—*a friend of the Brotherhood. An attractive, affluent woman, she owns the apartment where the narrator is introduced to the other members of the Brotherhood.*

Brother Hambro—*the man who trains the narrator in the art of rhetoric (argumentation and speechmaking).*

Brother Tarp—*a member of the Brotherhood's Harlem office. An older man, he is friendly to the narrator. His limp was caused by a traumatic incident in his past.*

Brother Tod Clifton—*another member of the Brotherhood. A charismatic young man, he comes to a dramatic and mysterious end.*

Brother Wrestrum—*a member of the Brotherhood who seems to oppose the narrator's career there.*

Brother Tobitt—*a member of the Brotherhood's Headquarters committee, whose sarcasm irritates the narrator. He takes a lead role in the accusations against the narrator.*

Hubert's wife—*an unnamed woman, with whom the narrator has an affair.*

Rinehart—*a shadowy local figure, both a criminal and a preacher, for whom the narrator is repeatedly mistaken.*

Brother Maceo—*one of the missing brothers. When the narrator finally finds Brother Maceo, he doesn't recognize him, because the narrator has on his "Rinehart disguise."*

Sybil—*the wife of one of the men in the organization. She and the narrator have an abortive affair.*

Dupre—*the leader of a bunch of looters, whom the narrator meets during the riots.*

Scofield—*one of the looters in the group.*

Summary of the Novel

Invisible Man is a first-person novel. It concerns an unnamed narrator, whom the reader meets in the Prologue. In the Epilogue, the narrator seems to "rejoin" the reader once again.

Other than his memories of his grandfather's death, the narrator reveals nothing about his childhood. After the humiliating battle royal (a chaotic boxing-match, along with sundry torments, in which high school boys competed), he goes to college, where he has an experience in betrayal that changes his life.

Having inadvertently taken an important visitor to the wrong places, the narrator is left exposed to the harsh judgment of Dr. Bledsoe, the president of the college. The narrator is emotionally scarred by what has happened.

Forced to leave the college that he loved, the narrator takes a bus to New York City to find work. There he tries to use letters of recommendation, but to no avail. He eventually takes a job in a paint factory. Another unpleasant lesson ensues there, for the narrator is untrained for the work. He is placed under the thumb of a bitter and distrusting man, who maneuvers the narrator into an industrial accident.

The narrator is once again torn loose from his moorings. After the accident, the narrator endured a bizarre experience, in which medical personnel tortured him. Mary, a stranger, finds the narrator in the street, and offers him a home. Soon afterward, a protest of the eviction of an old couple leads the narrator to join a political group called the Brotherhood.

The narrator seems to advance in the organization, but the petty politics and machinations of those around him ensure the narrator's instability. Eventually, the narrator is betrayed by the Brotherhood. Not long after one of the members is killed by a policeman, a riot begins. In the growing confusion, the narrator takes to the underground.

Estimated Reading Time

The average silent-reading rate for a secondary student is 250 to 300 words per minute, making the total reading time for this novel about 19 hours.

Invisible Man can be a challenging novel. Teachers will no doubt be sensitive to Ellison's subject matter and technique, and divide their assignments accordingly. Allow plenty of time to enjoy this great work. Reading the book according to the natural chapter breaks is the best approach, although most of the longer chapters have their own divisions.

SECTION TWO

Invisible Man

Prologue

New Character:

The narrator: *tells the story of his life, but remains unnamed*

Summary

The Prologue introduces the narrator with a monologue set inside the narrator's head. After having many adventures, which the reader will discover more about in the chapters to come, the narrator is resting and isolated. He uses the word "hibernation" to describe his status.

The Prologue begins with the narrator announcing that he is an invisible man. But he is also a man of substance—"flesh and bone, fiber and liquids"—not a creation of books or movies. In making clear that he is not literally invisible, the narrator proceeds to discuss what his invisibility is like, and how he has come to understand it.

The narrator describes his life, and the ways he interacts with others. One night, when the narrator feels that a man has refused to recognize his existence, he uses violence to force the man to admit that the narrator is there. Irrational as this scene may seem, it has its own logic. The narrator is convinced that the man never really saw him. The next day's newspaper seems to confirm his view. It calls the incident a mugging, even though the narrator hadn't tried to rob the man.

The narrator observes that there are also certain advantages to being ignored by white people. He lives in the basement of a whites-only building and diverts free electricity for the many (1,369) lightbulbs he has plugged in.

At the same time, the narrator is aware of his aloneness, and no amount of irony and cynicism will conceal his loneliness. He talks about "re-entering" society. He makes no distinction between white society and black society, having proved to himself that his invisibility is equally effective in both.

The narrator mentions characters such as Brother Jack, Ras, and Rinehart, whom the reader will meet later in the novel.

Analysis

The Prologue introduces a sharp mind that has suffered a great deal. The reader may think that the narrator is not sane, considering he attacks a man for not noticing him. However it is too early to tell, and we must judge him by his words, actions, and past.

The narrator tends to express himself indirectly. His fantastic imagination provides a crucial clue to his unhappiness. At one point, he says that his feelings of ambivalence are the cause of his being where he is.

The narrator's estrangement from society has made him an observer rather than a participant. He views people from a distance, from his alienated vantage point, often seeing in human behavior what other people do not notice. Unfortunately, learning about people in this way does not seem to help the narrator find what he spends the novel searching for. The humor that the narrator uses is dark and cynical.

Study Questions

1. What does the narrator tell us about himself in the very beginning of the prologue?
2. To what does the narrator attribute his invisibility?
3. Why does the narrator attack a man in the street?
4. What is the name of the company with which the narrator claims to be "having a fight"?

Prologue

5. What reason does the narrator give for his fight with this company?
6. Whose music does the narrator enjoy?
7. What is described in the first part of the narrator's fantasy?
8. When the narrator talks to the old woman in his fantasy, what reason does she give for loving her old master?
9. Why does one of the old woman's sons attack the narrator in the fantasy?
10. What has the narrator done to make his dwelling-place more livable?

Answers

1. The narrator says that he is an invisible man. He next says that he is a flesh-and-blood man, not a creation of writers or film directors.
2. The narrator attributes his invisibility to the failure on the part of the eyes of other people to see him.
3. The narrator attacks a man in the street because the man fails to apologize for insulting him, thereby not acknowledging the narrator's existence.
4. The name of the company with which the narrator is having a fight is Monopolated Light & Power.
5. The narrator says that he fights with Monopolated Light & Power to feel his "vital aliveness."
6. The narrator enjoys the music of Louis Armstrong.
7. The first part of the narrator's fantasy is a sermon.
8. When the narrator talks to the old woman in his fantasy, she says that she loved her old master because he gave her several sons.
9. One of the old woman's sons attacks the narrator in the fantasy because the narrator made the man's mother cry by asking her too many questions.

10. To make his dwelling-place more livable, the narrator has installed a great number of lightbulbs. He has 1,369, and says that he plans to put in many more.

Suggested Essay Topics

1. What does the reader know about the narrator solely on the basis of the Prologue? Take this opportunity to play detective, and explain both what he reveals about himself explicitly and what inferences can be drawn, justifying your findings as you go along.
2. Focus on the fantasy section of the Prologue. What's going on there? The narrator imagines a series of scenes beginning with a sermon. What themes does it reveal?

Chapter One

New Characters:

Grandfather: *not an actual character, although his dying words greatly disturb the narrator*

Jackson: *a particularly sadistic member of the audience at the battle royal*

Tatlock: *a large and vicious boy whom the narrator is forced to fight during the battle royal*

Summary

A brief anecdote about the narrator's grandfather begins the chapter. Through his childhood and early adulthood, the narrator is confused by his grandfather's "deathbed curse." After the narrator gives his high school graduation speech on humility, he is invited to give his speech before a special audience. At this event, the narrator realizes that young men from the local black high school have been brought together for the sadistic amusement of white men.

Chapter 1

First, a naked white woman dances in front of the high school students. The strong emotions generated by such a forbidden sight are channelled into a free-for-all boxing match. The narrator faces Tatlock, who is filled with rage. The distribution of prize money provides more torture.

Finally, the narrator makes his speech. The audience, at first not really listening, changes when the narrator says "social equality" instead of "social responsibility." Despite this difficulty, the narrator finishes with applause and a prize. The superintendent presents him with a new briefcase, containing a scholarship to an all-black state college.

Analysis

The story of the narrator's grandfather frames the narrator's central struggle: the line between honesty and insanity. The adults react to the grandfather's "deathbed curse," as the narrator sometimes calls it, by saying that the grandfather was crazy. This is hardly the only possibility. The question of whether or not many of the characters are crazy runs through the entire novel.

The fact that the whole of the narrator's life before college is reduced to one evening suggests that the story of that evening, which he calls the battle royal, can serve as an indication of something greater. Although the characters in the first chapter do not reappear in the novel, the battle royal provides the reader with crucial insights. Similarly, though Jackson and Tatlock are flat characters, they embody important facets of home to the narrator.

The whites look at their victims as entertainment, not individuals. Tatlock represents the distortions of relationships between blacks in the presence of whites. Why does Tatlock fight so hard? Most likely because his situation with the whites makes him angry, and the narrator is the only person on whom Tatlock can vent his rage.

An intense atmosphere of malice and instability pervades the battle royal. Ellison effectively blends comedy and fantastical imagery with drama and pathos. For example, the description of the blond dancer suggests a fragile, magical being, instead of the sordid pawn that torments them. At the same time, many of the details of the battle royal are highly realistic.

Chapter 1

Study Questions

1. How do the adults respond to the grandfather's deathbed speech?
2. Where does the battle royal take place?
3. What kinds of men does the narrator see in the audience?
4. What does the blond woman have tattooed on her belly?
5. How is the boxing match made more entertaining for the audience?
6. How does the narrator try to appease Tatlock when the two are boxing?
7. How do the whites first try to pay the young men for their boxing?
8. Are the coins real?
9. What happens when the narrator accepts the briefcase presented to him?
10. Who is in the dream the narrator has at the end of the chapter?

Answers

1. When the grandfather spoke his dying words, the adults around his deathbed rushed the young children from the room, drew the shades, and lowered the flames on the oil lamps. They were frightened and embarrassed.
2. The battle royal takes place in the ballroom of a large hotel.
3. The narrator sees the town's leading bankers, lawyers, judges, doctors, teachers, and even a pastor in the audience.
4. The blond woman has an American flag tattooed on her belly.
5. The audience makes the boxing match more entertaining by blindfolding the boxers.
6. The narrator tries to appease Tatlock by offering to split the prize money with him. This tactic does not work.

7. When the white men first offer "gold coins" to the boxers, they drop them on a piece of rug. The rug carries electrical current, and all of the boys receive shocks.
8. No, the coins are not real. They turn out to be brass tokens, advertisements for a kind of automobile.
9. When the narrator accepts the briefcase, a liquid rope of blood and saliva leaves his mouth, dripping on the new leather.
10. The narrator's grandfather is in the dream at the end of the chapter, laughing at the narrator.

Suggested Essay Topics
1. Why might the adults present at grandfather's deathbed have reacted the way that they did? If it's true that the grandfather may have been crazy, what other possibilities exist?
2. Why would the audience listening to the narrator's speech have reacted so strongly to the narrator's mistake? Discuss the implications of his slip of the tongue.

Chapter Two

New Characters:

Mr. Norton: *the rich white northern benefactor whom the narrator chauffeurs in a college-owned car*

Jim Trueblood: *the poor sharecropper who tells Mr. Norton a story*

Summary
The narrator drives Mr. Norton along the quiet roadways of the campus where the narrator attends college. The nervous narrator is reassured by Mr. Norton's confidence and curiosity about the narrator's future. Mr. Norton and the narrator also talk about Mr. Norton's daughter, who died suddenly and mysteriously.

After a few chance turns, they reach an area of old cabins. The

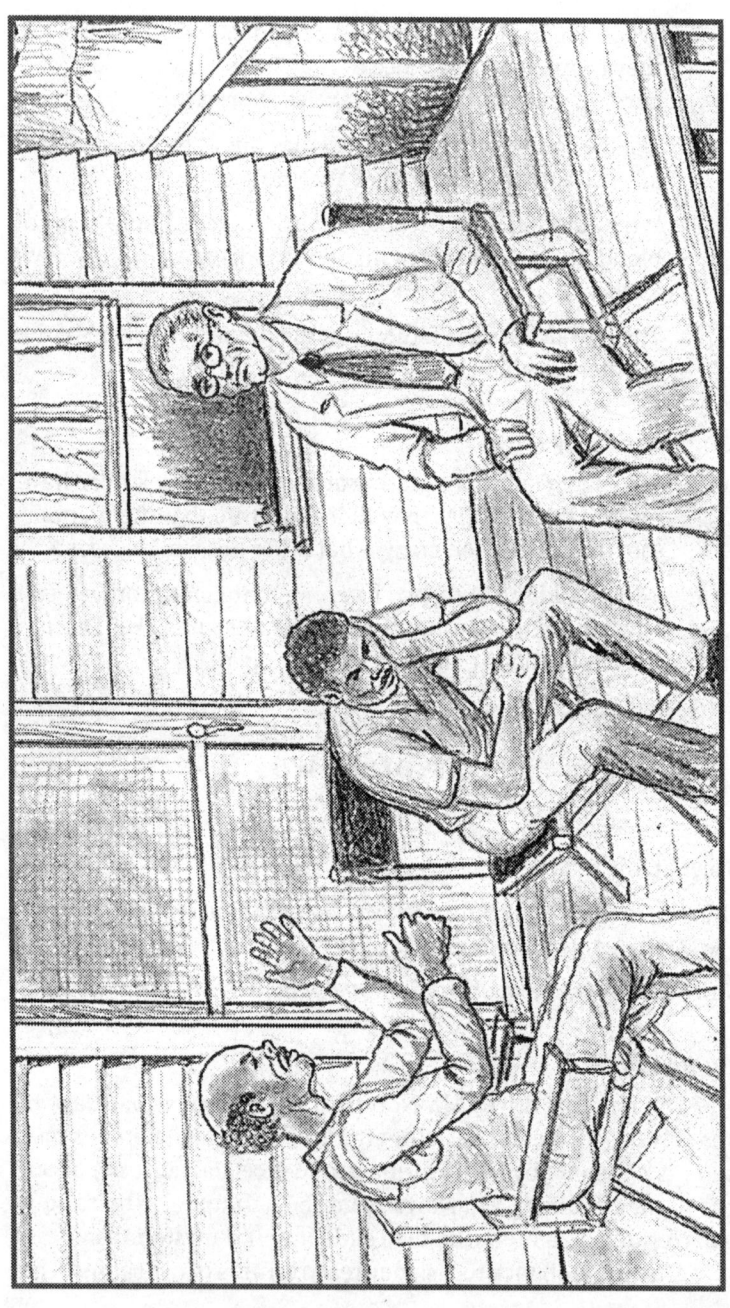

Chapter 2

narrator repeats what is told about Jim Trueblood, owner of one of the cabins—that he had had a child with his own daughter. Despite the narrator's reluctance, Mr. Norton insists on talking with Jim Trueblood.

Jim Trueblood tells them the story, saying that he never meant to sleep with his daughter, Matty Lou. As he fell asleep in their single bed, he had been thinking about a woman he'd known years before. This, combined with his strange and erotic dream, made him lose control of himself. When his wife saw the "accident" taking place, she tried to kill him for his sin.

The narrator is repulsed and disgusted by the story. Mr. Norton is transfixed, and so dangerously upset that the wondering narrator must suddenly fear for Mr. Norton's health.

Analysis

This chapter's opening paragraphs focus on the quiet beauty of the campus, communicating a sense of loss. The reader cannot be sure that the narrator was successful there.

Even at this black college, indebtedness to whites is present. One of the benefactors of the college, Mr. Norton is there for Founder's Day; ironically, the whiteness or blackness of the Founder is never disclosed.

Assigned to chauffeur Mr. Norton, the narrator, despite his awe of Mr. Norton, allows a truth-related catastrophe to occur. The fact that Mr. Norton hears, and is deeply upset by, Jim Trueblood's story is sure to have its consequences for the narrator.

Study Questions

1. What writer does Mr. Norton talk about with the narrator?
2. Does the narrator tell Mr. Norton when the cabins were built?
3. What are Jim Trueblood and his family doing when the college car arrives?
4. Is there any point at which the narrator can avoid bringing Mr. Norton and Jim Trueblood together?
5. Who most wants to meet Jim Trueblood, the narrator or Mr. Norton?

6. Does Jim Trueblood say that he and his family have been mistreated by the local whites?
7. What does Jim Trueblood say the college has done for them?
8. Does Mr. Norton give Jim Trueblood any money?
9. What game are Jim Trueblood's little children playing?
10. What does Mr. Norton ask the narrator for at the end of the chapter?

Answers

1. Mr. Norton talks about Ralph Waldo Emerson with the narrator.
2. Yes, the narrator tells Mr. Norton that the cabins were built in the time of slavery.
3. When the college car arrives, Jim Trueblood and his family are washing clothes in a large pot over a fire.
4. Yes, there were several moments in which the narrator, by simply not telling Mr. Norton the whole story about Jim Trueblood, could have avoided the meeting.
5. Mr. Norton insists on getting out of the car to meet Jim Trueblood. The narrator is not at all happy about the idea.
6. No, Jim Trueblood does not say that he and his family have been mistreated by the local whites. In fact, they have been helped out quite a bit by white people recently.
7. Jim Trueblood tells Mr. Norton and the narrator that the college has tried to push them off their land, and make them move away.
8. Mr. Norton gives Jim Trueblood a hundred-dollar bill.
9. Jim Trueblood's little children are playing "London Bridge is Falling Down."
10. Mr. Norton asks the narrator to get him "a little stimulant," meaning alcohol, at the end of the chapter.

Chapter 3 19

Suggested Essay Topics
1. Examine the details the narrator gives about the college at the start of the chapter. What kind of picture is evoked? What do we know about that part of the narrator's life?
2. Notice how the narrator is determined to show Mr. Norton something he'd never seen before. Follow the progression of statements, thoughts, and decisions bringing Mr. Norton and Jim Trueblood together.

Chapter Three

New Characters:

Big Halley: *a bartender at the Golden Day*

Sylvester: *a mental patient and a patron of the Golden Day*

Supercargo: *the attendant/warden at the Golden Day*

The Vet: *a strange little man who tends to Mr. Norton's condition upstairs; The talk that the two of them have puts the Vet in a vulnerable position.*

Edna: *a prostitute at the Golden Day. She shows great interest in spending more time with Mr. Norton.*

Summary

The car arrives at the Golden Day, a bar and whorehouse. Mr. Norton requires "a stimulant," in the form of alcohol, to overcome the shock of Jim Trueblood's story. Mr. Norton's condition is unknown, but his aristocratic constitution implies a certain delicacy.

The stumbling men in front of the car are the veterans and mental incompetents that make the Golden Day a rowdy place. The narrator knows that this was not a good place to bring Mr. Norton, but going to town would have taken too long.

The narrator tries to get Halley, the bartender, to give him a drink for Mr. Norton. When Halley refuses, the narrator goes out

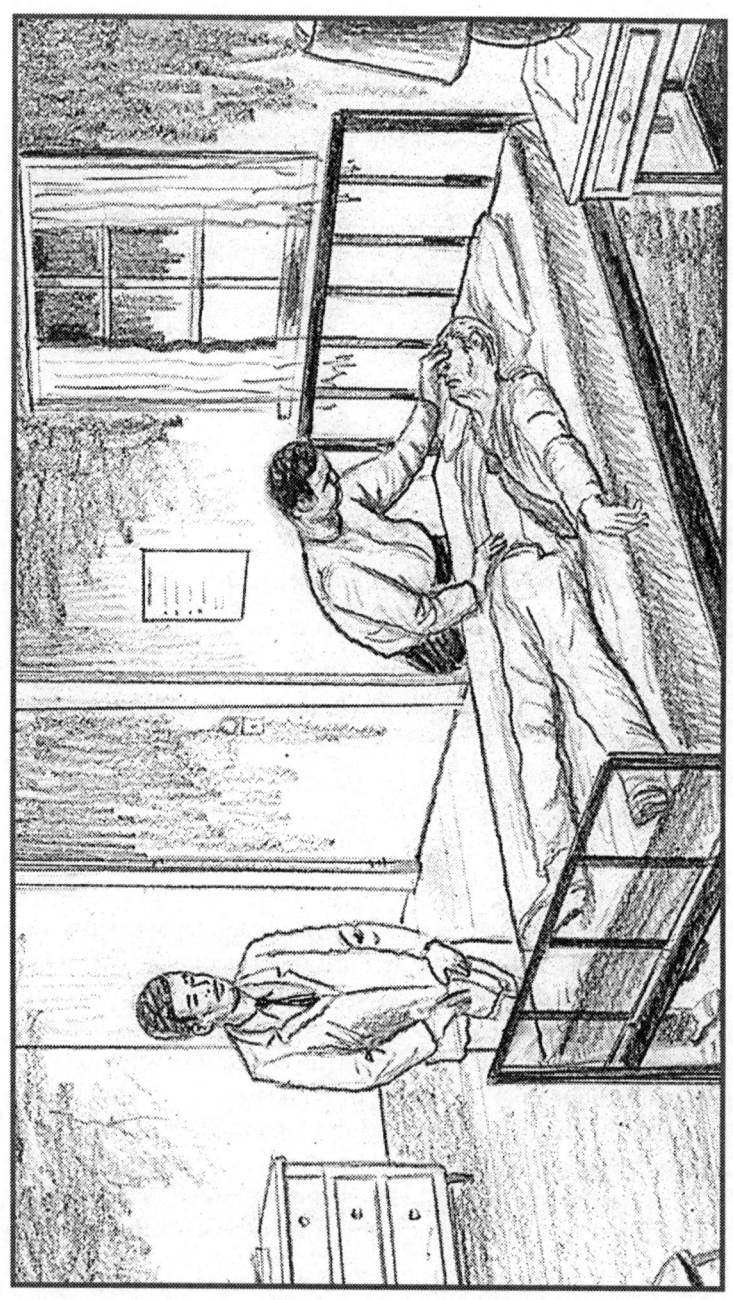

Chapter 3

to the car, and finds that Mr. Norton has fainted. Sylvester and another man help bring Mr. Norton inside. Someone slaps Mr. Norton across the face to revive him, and a drink is administered.

Just after Mr. Norton awakens, Supercargo enters the scene. Being the attendant in charge of these men, he is accustomed to being in command. Now, however, everyone is affected by alcohol, and Supercargo's threatening presence so angers the men that they attack him.

Supercargo is overcome and severely beaten. It is soon clear that Mr. Norton would be safer upstairs. Once there, the Vet continues treating Mr. Norton, and the three of them engage in a long conversation, which continues until the narrator's and Mr. Norton's angery departure.

Analysis

Whether or not he intends to, the narrator continues to do what he did in the previous chapter—to confront Mr. Norton with the day-to-day realities of black life in the South. He has brought Mr. Norton to two places that those in the college react to with embarrassment and anger.

While the chaos in this chapter is as intense as the battle royal in Chapter One, the reasons behind it are different. The Golden Day has its own strange sense of logic; the men do not have to deal with white people, and their "craziness" keeps them out of trouble. The situation with Supercargo, however, angers them. They say they cannot speak freely when he is present, which means that he treats them the way a white man would. They make him pay dearly for that crime. They are not afraid of Mr. Norton, but they have no desire to hurt him; that would mean real trouble.

The Vet's short speeches may seem confusing. Some of what he says is indirectly stated, as the narrator himself has done in the Prologue. The vet says that he had forgotten things he never should have forgotten; the whites might have said that the Vet "forgot his place." In learning medicine and healing, the Vet neglected to keep in mind the realities of American racism. Other statements the vet makes sound completely crazy, but, as usual, this is not necessarily the case.

Study Questions

1. Whose car does the narrator claim to be driving, in order to get the veterans out of the way?
2. Why does Halley refuse to give or sell the narrator a drink?
3. Who does Sylvester claim that Mr. Norton was?
4. What kind of alcohol is given to Mr. Norton?
5. In his excitement, what does the narrator have an urge to do when he sees Supercargo being beaten?
6. Why does the Vet send the narrator out of the room where he is treating Mr. Norton?
7. Where did the Vet receive his medical training?
8. What surprises Mr. Norton about the Vet's medical knowledge?
9. How does Mr. Norton summarize the man who had tended his condition?
10. Do the narrator and Mr. Norton have any difficulties upon leaving the Golden Day?

Answers

1. In order to get the veterans out of the road, the narrator claims that he has General Pershing in the car.
2. Halley refuses to allow the narrator to bring a drink outside because there are some people who are trying to shut his place down, he says.
3. As he helps bring Mr. Norton into the Golden Day, Sylvester claims that Mr. Norton is the former's grandfather.
4. Mr. Norton is given a drink from Halley's private brandy stock.
5. When he sees Supercargo being beaten, the narrator felt such a feeling of excitement that he wants to join in.
6. The Vet sends the narrator out of the room to get a glass of water.

7. The Vet received his medical training in France.
8. Mr. Norton is surprised to find that the Vet reached the same diagnosis as the former's own specialist.
9. Mr. Norton says that "the man is as insane as all the rest."
10. Yes, the narrator and Mr. Norton do have some difficulty in leaving the Golden Day. First, Edna says that she doesn't want "white folks" to leave. Then Mr. Norton falls once again, scraping his head on the screen door.

Suggested Essay Topics
1. We are told that the men who visit the Golden Day are "shell-shocked," which means that they are suffering from permanent stress from wartime battles. What other reasons might they have for being there?
2. The prolonged scene of chaos that unfolds inside the Golden Day is comparable with the descriptions of the battle royal. What are the differences? Look at the relationships between the people involved. What different purposes does the violence serve?

Chapter Four

New Character:

Dr. Bledsoe: *the president of the college*

Summary

Upon returning to campus, the narrator drops Mr. Norton off and goes to see Dr. Bledsoe, the president of the college. Feeling certain that he will be blamed for having subjected Mr. Norton to both Jim Trueblood's story and the events at the Golden Day, the narrator is in an agony of nervousness.

Dr. Bledsoe is greatly disconcerted by the course of events, and, despite Mr. Norton's words to the contrary, does indeed blame the narrator. The narrator is ordered to see Dr. Bledsoe later that evening, after attending a campus church service. Both on the way to his room, and once having arrived there, the narrator is accosted by fellow students, whose blithe chatter further strains the narrator's nerves.

Analysis

In this chapter, the narrator becomes aware of the danger he faces. Having broken unwritten rules, he expects a severe penalty for what he has done, although this is unconfirmed. The narrator does not realize that his not having done anything will not make any difference.

Ellison makes good use of suspense. Although the character telling the story has already lived through it and knows what happened, the resolution of the narrator's fears are withheld from the reader, who is kept in suspense along with the young man in the memory.

This is far more effective than if the narrator had told us what happened, and then explained how that conclusion came into being. The chronology of the day's events (remember that this day started in Chapter Two and is not yet over) is meticulously followed.

There is little large-scale drama here, as we saw at the Golden Day. Instead, more subtle clues tell the reader about the characters. For example, the narrator notices the extent to which Dr. Bledsoe changes when he is with Mr. Norton. The reader has an opportunity to see how Dr. Bledsoe acts toward the narrator.

Study Questions

1. What do the narrator and Mr. Norton talk about on the way back to the college campus?
2. Whom does the narrator blame for his predicament?
3. Who does Mr. Norton ask the narrator to bring to him?
4. What is Dr. Bledsoe's nickname?
5. What is Dr. Bledsoe doing when the narrator comes into his office?

Chapter 4

6. Does Mr. Norton try to blame the narrator for what has happened?
7. What is the password that a young woman asks the narrator to carry to her boyfriend?
8. Does anyone try to kid around with the narrator?
9. In his extreme gratitude, whom does the narrator imagine Mr. Norton to seem like?
10. In a discussion of Emerson, what virtue is briefly mentioned?

Answers

1. The narrator and Mr. Norton do not talk about anything on the way back to the college campus.
2. The narrator blames Jim Trueblood for his (the narrator's) predicament.
3. Mr. Norton asks the narrator to bring Dr. Bledsoe and the school physician to him.
4. Dr. Bledsoe's nickname is "Old Bucket-Head."
5. Dr. Bledsoe is on the phone when the narrator comes into his office, presumably trying to find the narrator and Mr. Norton.
6. No, Mr. Norton does not try to blame the narrator for what happened. He specifically says that the narrator was not at fault.
7. The young woman asks the narrator to carry the message "the grass is green" to her boyfriend.
8. Yes, someone does try to kid around with the narrator. While the narrator is waiting to go to chapel, his roommate enters and tries to joke with the disconsolate narrator.
9. In his highly emotional state, the narrator imagines Mr. Norton to be like St. Nicholas (Santa Claus).
10. The virtue of self-reliance comes into the conversation about Emerson.

Suggested Essay Topics

1. Write a character sketch of Dr. Bledsoe based on the information in this chapter. What does the reader know about him? What inferences can be drawn from this knowledge? Be sure to support your observations.

2. Summarize the narrator's "crimes," as Dr. Bledsoe might call them. Explain how they happened, and whether or not the narrator could have avoided them. Who is right in this situation?

Chapter Five

New Character:

The Reverend Homer A. Barbee: *the man who gives the sermon the narrator hears in this chapter; Barbee provides a perspective of hollow pride and rhetoric.*

Summary

As ordered by Dr. Bledsoe, the narrator goes to the college chapel. Before the evening's guest speaker begins his sermon, the narrator meditates upon his own precarious status. He then recalls the times that he spoke publicly at the college.

He returns to the present scene, describing the people there, including Dr. Bledsoe. There is a choir solo and the sermon begins, praising the lives and visions of those who built the college.

The sermon is delivered by Reverend Homer A. Barbee, of Chicago. Its topic is the great work of making the college, accomplished by the godlike yet entirely humble personalities of the Founder and Dr. Bledsoe. Barbee works the crowd and uses techniques of oratory to make the story into an epic saga of heroism. The narrator, moved and demoralized, is left feeling like a traitor. He dreads all the more his imminent talk with Dr. Bledsoe.

Chapter 5

Analysis

This is a difficult chapter, because little actually happens. Instead, the first half of the chapter takes place entirely inside the narrator's head. Moreover, the narrator is doing two things at once: he is reliving the evening, as well as remembering the evening from the perspective of a grown man.

The narrator sits in the college chapel, waiting for both the guest speaker to deliver his sermon, and, more importantly, for an answer from Dr. Bledsoe about the consequences of the day's unfortunate events.

While waiting for the sermon, the narrator examines his situation, savoring all its exquisite details of beauty and anguish. The meditation on his life in college, which he looks upon as lost, leads him to recall moments when he too stood upon the church-stage and spoke oratorically. This is the section printed in italic type, where the narrator throws words around in a sort of celebration of their uselessness.

One might say that there are three sermons in the chapter. The narrator gives two personal sermons before the official one commences.

The chapter begins with descriptions of nature and landscape in which all the senses are invoked. It is reminiscent of the start of the second chapter; the narrator is holding onto details in a loving fashion.

Also, the beginning of the chapter contains a shift in tense, from past to present. This shift, in the second sentence of the chapter, makes the narrator's perceptions more immediate and dramatic. It indicates that these perceptions are frozen in time; the narrator we met in the prologue is reliving the event.

Study Questions

1. What signal tells the narrator that it is time to go to the chapel?
2. What is Dr. Bledsoe wearing to the chapel on this evening?
3. What is Dr. Bledsoe able to do that fascinated the narrator?

4. To whom does Dr. Bledsoe give a secret signal?

5. How does the narrator describe the speaker of the sermon?

6. What catastrophe does the speaker say almost ended Dr. Bledsoe's life?

7. Who tells the narrator the speaker's name?

8. In what northern city does the Reverend Barbee preach?

9. What does the narrator notice about the Reverend Barbee at the end of his sermon?

10. Does the narrator stay to hear the other speakers?

Answers

1. The sound of the vesper-bells is the signal that tells the narrator that it is time to go to the chapel.

2. Dr. Bledsoe is wearing striped trousers, a swallow-tail coat with fancy black-braided lapels, and an ascot tie.

3. The narrator is fascinated by the way that Dr. Bledsoe touches the white visitors, shaking their hands or putting his hand on their arms.

4. Dr. Bledsoe gives a secret signal to the organist.

5. The narrator describes the speaker of the sermon as "a man of striking ugliness; fat, with a bullet head set on a short neck."

6. The speaker says that an "insane cousin splashed the infant Dr. Bledsoe with lye, and that he lay in a coma for nine days before miraculously coming out of it."

7. A fellow student tells the narrator, in an annoyed, outraged manner, that the speaker is the Reverend Homer A. Barbee.

8. The Reverend Barbee preaches in Chicago.

9. At the end of Reverend Barbee's sermon, the narrator learns that the reverend is blind.

10. No, the narrator does not stay to hear the other speakers, but the service is over immediately after he leaves the chapel.

Suggested Essay Topics

1. The Founder is an important figure in the sermon. Does Reverend Barbee disclose the race of the Founder? By what information can the reader divine whether the Founder was black or white? What difference would this have made?

2. At the end of the chapter, the narrator feels that the sermon is not likely to make Dr. Bledsoe soft-hearted when considering the narrator's situation. Why does the narrator feel this way? How might Dr. Bledsoe's mood be influenced by the sermon? What about the sermon would create this mood?

Chapter Six

Summary

After some last-minute panic and forestalling, the narrator has his interview with Dr. Bledsoe. Though the conversation begins pleasantly, it changes suddenly when the college president heaps abuse upon the narrator. Then Dr. Bledsoe tells the narrator his decision. The narrator is dismissed from college.

The narrator's first response is outrage and anger. This shocks and then amuses Dr. Bledsoe, who says the narrator is powerless. When it comes right down to it, the narrator does not really exist, because he does not matter. The college president tells the narrator about how a person gets power, and what it means to have it.

Dr. Bledsoe tells the narrator that he will give him some letters to help him find work, and that the narrator has a short period of time to end his affairs.

The narrator leaves the office and vomits. He thinks about going back home, and the reactions he would face from those still there. He decides that Dr. Bledsoe's decision was correct, and that he must accept his fate. He gets ready to leave.

Dr. Bledsoe is displeased to see the narrator the next morning, until the narrator says that he would like to get going and asks for the letters that Dr. Bledsoe had mentioned the night before. After collecting them, the narrator catches a bus.

Chapter 6

Analysis

The reader has long been anticipating the confrontation between the narrator and Dr. Bledsoe. It is very dramatic, but not highly surprising. The narrator was expecting to be expelled.

Ellison is very skilled at capturing the tension of this meeting. The narrator receives a lesson on how power involves deception. The reader is getting a similar lesson on the forces that made the narrator into the invisible man who introduced himself in the Prologue.

The narrator feels powerless in front of Dr. Bledsoe. He does not leave the office immediately, as he had been ready to do. Instead, he stays and listens, angry at himself for doing so, and filled with an agony of hate and confused fear.

One of the issues in this chapter is honesty. Dr. Bledsoe accuses the narrator of lying to him, and castigates the narrator for not lying to Mr. Norton. At the same time, Dr. Bledsoe tells the narrator not to treat him like a white man, even while calling the narrator a "nigger." This puts the narrator in a sort of double bind, for Dr. Bledsoe is exerting power over the narrator just as a white man would do, even while telling the narrator that he has pulled the race down into the mud.

Study Questions

1. What is the narrator shocked and deeply hurt to hear Dr. Bledsoe call him?
2. What object does Dr. Bledsoe lift from the desk, from under a pile of papers?
3. How does the narrator respond when Dr. Bledsoe tells him that he will have to leave the college?
4. How does Dr. Bledsoe respond to the narrator's response?
5. How much time does Dr. Bledsoe give the narrator to settle his affairs?
6. What does the narrator do as soon as he returns to his room?
7. How much money does the narrator have in his savings?
8. Why does the narrator return to Dr. Bledsoe's office twice

more at the end of the chapter?
9. What warning does Dr. Bledsoe give the narrator concerning the letters?
10. How many letters is the narrator given?

Answers
1. The narrator is shocked and deeply hurt to hear Dr. Bledsoe call him a "nigger."
2. Dr. Bledsoe lifts an old iron shackle, the kind used in slavery days, from underneath the pile of papers on the desk.
3. When Dr. Bledsoe tells the narrator that he will have to leave, the latter responds very angrily, saying he will go to Mr. Norton and tell him everything.
4. Dr. Bledsoe responds to the narrator's response with great amusement.
5. Dr. Bledsoe gives the narrator two days to settle his affairs.
6. As soon as he returns to his room, the narrator counts the money in his savings.
7. The narrator has about fifty dollars in his savings.
8. The narrator goes to Dr. Bledsoe's office twice more, near the end of the chapter, first to tell Dr. Bledsoe he plans to leave the next morning, rather than use the whole two days that were allowed him, and last to receive the letters that Dr. Bledsoe promised him.
9. Dr. Bledsoe warns the narrator not to open the letters himself, or try to read them in any way.
10. The narrator is given seven letters.

Suggested Essay Topics
1. Consider Dr. Bledsoe's way of looking at race relations. He tells the narrator that it didn't matter what Mr. Norton wanted to see or do; the narrator was in charge. Bledsoe also says that he thought that the narrator had more sense and

was not such a fool. What were Dr. Bledsoe's expectations of the narrator? How does he suggest that the narrator could have lied? How did the narrator fail to meet those expectations?

2. At one point in their talk, Dr. Bledsoe says that Mr. Norton could have made the narrator's fortune. What does this mean and imply? Consider the relative positions of the narrator and Mr. Norton, and the fact that the narrator thinks about the possibility of getting something from Mr. Norton at the beginning of Chapter Two. What would the narrator have had to do in order to get something from Mr. Norton, and why was he unable to do it?

Chapter Seven

New Characters:

Crenshaw: *the man in charge of getting the vet to his new home*

Ras (later known as "Ras the Exhorter"): *the leader of a political group in Harlem*

Summary

The narrator takes a bus from campus, beginning the next part of his life. He carries letters of introduction from Dr. Bledsoe. Two other men are traveling that day—the Vet (the inmate from the Golden Day that provided medical aid to Mr. Norton), and Crenshaw, the Vet's attendant.

Before the two transfer to another bus, the Vet again comments on the narrator's situation. Once in New York, the narrator sees the very different lives that blacks can lead in a big northern city.

Analysis

Once again, the reader comes to the question of whether or not the Vet is crazy. Actually, he seems quite lucid and makes a lot of sense. Then why is he going off to a mental institution?

Chapter 7

Although the narrator has just recently been torn away from the life he knew and loved, he is no longer depressed by the end of the chapter. We have the feeling that everything is new for the narrator. His confusion holds far more excitement than fear.

The reader is introduced to a new stage of the narrator's life and may well feel a similar kind of excitement. The introduction of Ras is important to this chapter. He illustrates a new response to the white America portrayed in the novel and a new kind of politics.

Study Questions

1. Does the narrator have much choice other than to sit with the Vet and Crenshaw?
2. To whom does the narrator compare Crenshaw?
3. What changes does the Vet imagine when he thinks of the narrator's life in Harlem?
4. How does the Vet feel about his transfer?
5. What does Crenshaw say to the Vet to make him stop "showing off"?
6. How does the narrator feel when Crenshaw and the Vet transfer to another bus?
7. What disturbing experience does the narrator have in the subway soon after arriving in New York City?
8. Along with the revelation that blacks in Harlem have jobs and economic power, what specific event completely shocks the narrator?
9. What does the narrator notice, and commment upon, regarding Ras?
10. What decision does the narrator come to about Harlem at the end of the chapter?

Answers

1. No, the narrator does not have much choice other than to sit with the Vet and Crenshaw. The back of the bus is the only section available to them.

2. The narrator compares Crenshaw to Supercargo, the attendant at the Golden Day.

3. The Vet imagines the narrator going to lectures at the Men's House and meeting more white people—perhaps even a white girl.

4. The Vet is a little confused about his transfer. He says that he had been trying to get transferred for a long time, and then it happens soon after meeting Mr. Norton.

5. Crenshaw, impatient with the Vet, accuses him of showing off his education. Crenshaw reminds the Vet that he is still riding "in the Jim Crow," the back of the bus, just as Crenshaw himself is.

6. When Crenshaw and the Vet transfer to another bus, the narrator heaves a sigh of relief, but then feels sad and alone.

7. The narrator is crammed into a crowded subway car, soon after his arrival in New York City, and pressed against a large, white woman.

8. Along with the revelation that blacks in Harlem have jobs and economic power, the narrator is completely shocked to see a public demonstration of political protest by Ras. What also stuns the narrator is the fact that two white police officers make no attempt to stop the protest.

9. The narrator notices and comments upon the West Indian accent in Ras.

10. At the end of the chapter, having registered in his room at the Men's house, the narrator decides that he will have to get used to Harlem a little at a time.

Suggested Essay Topics

1. It is important to remember what Dr. Bledsoe said about the Vet (hint: look about five pages into Chapter Six). Is it a coincidence that the Vet is going up to St. Elizabeth's? Why would someone like Dr. Bledsoe want the vet to be sent away?

2. Describe the narrator's impressions of both New York City

and Harlem. What is different about his new surroundings, and what changes will they most likely lead to in the narrator's life?

Chapter Eight

Summary

The narrator starts to get to know the city, and begins his search for a job, using the letters. He is plagued by his expectations and fears, but is still fascinated by this new world.

In the first of the huge offices where he delivers his letters, the narrator talks with a receptionist. The narrator wonders whether the reactions he is getting are racially motivated, but decides that they are not. Alone and worried, the narrator hopes for a change.

Analysis

The narrator's energies, which were high when he first arrived in New York, are flagging. His feelings of isolation and persecution are increased by his poor prospects for a job.

He dreams about his bright future, and the ways that he will conduct himself as a successful man. The narrator has done this before—retreat into a fantasy world when he is in doubt—in the Prologue.

The day dreams, and the movies to which he goes to keep himself cheerful, do not work. He begins to feel that there is something about him that people notice. He says that his clothes feel ill-fitting.

Study Questions

1. What book does the narrator find in his room?
2. What memories does the book awaken?
3. What does the narrator briefly consider doing with the letters?
4. Where does the narrator ride the subway to the next morning?

5. To whose office does the narrator go?
6. What is the man's receptionist like?
7. Is the narrator able to meet the man he went to see?
8. What are one or two of the narrator's specific worries?
9. To which two people does the narrator write letters?
10. What ray of hope does the narrator receive at the end of the chapter?

Answers
1. The narrator finds a Gideon Bible in his room.
2. The Bible awakens memories of both Dr. Bledsoe quoting from it during speeches, and of family prayer around the dinner table.
3. The narrator briefly considers trying to steam the letters open.
4. The narrator takes the subway to the Wall Street district.
5. The narrator first goes to Mr. Bates' office.
6. The receptionist at Mr. Bates' office is a young woman, whom the narrator summarizes as "kind and interested," though he had expected that she would act antagonistically toward him.
7. No, the narrator is not able to meet Mr. Bates, who is too busy to see him.
8. The narrator is specifically worried about his lack of money, and by lingering thoughts that Dr. Bledsoe and Mr. Norton were somehow acting against him.
9. The narrator writes letters to Mr. Emerson and to Mr. Norton.
10. The narrator receives a ray of hope at the end of the chapter in the form of a letter from Mr. Emerson.

Suggested Essay Topics
1. Summarize the narrator's fears. Are they reasonable, given

what you have read in the novel? If the fears center on Dr. Bledsoe and Mr. Norton, are there grounds for the narrator to be concerned? If the fears are based on other feelings, is there evidence behind them?

2. In this chapter and the one before it, the narrator saw black people with jobs unlike those that blacks had in the south. Pick three examples and describe them. What responsibilities do these jobs involve? What does it imply to say that blacks can and do hold them?

Chapter Nine

New Character:

Mr. Emerson's Son: *the man with whom the narrator has an unsuccessful interview*

Summary

On his way to an important interview, the narrator meets with people who shake his sense of identity. At Mr. Emerson's office, the narrator delivers his letter and is asked to wait. After a pause, the narrator converses with the man who took the narrator's letter.

The conversation begins amicably, but deteriorates as the narrator grows uneasy. After much confusion, the man shows the narrator the letter from Dr. Bledsoe. Stating that the narrator was an embarrassment to the college, the letter asks Mr. Emerson to please shun the narrator and his request for employment.

The narrator is devastated, but maintains his composure. The man's offers of employment are politely declined, and the narrator leaves.

Soon after, the narrator finds his anger. After considering that young Emerson might have been lying somehow, he broods on the subject of Dr. Bledsoe. His emotions run between laughter and blind rage.

Analysis

Although the narrator's encounters with the blueprint man and the counterman are only momentary, they nonetheless signify a great deal. Both men show their feelings that the narrator might be acting to conceal what they consider his "true self."

The narrator acknowledges this possibility, and senses that to deny his heritage would be dishonest. Yet this is a gray area, in which no one is right or wrong. After all, are the men right to have these expectations? Is the narrator obligated to have certain preferences, or to behave in a certain way, because of where and how he grew up? The narrator may or may not be stifling who he is. Questions regarding the honest expressions of identity remain unanswered.

In the narrator's conversation with Mr. Emerson's son, the reader sees the potential for dialogue between the races. Both the narrator's mistrust and the young Emerson's inner conflictedness prevent any real communication.

Study Questions

1. How does the narrator describe the day at the start of the chapter?
2. What does the short-order cook assume that the narrator would like to eat?
3. What does the blueprint man ask the narrator?
4. What book does the narrator see open in the office?
5. What does the narrator decide about the men who operate this firm, based on what he sees in their plush office?
6. What does the man ask the narrator that makes the latter's mind "begin to whirl," as the narrator puts it?
7. In the midst of talking with the man, whose words of advice and caution does the narrator remember?
8. Who does the man the narrator is talking with turn out to be?
9. At the end of their conversation, what does the man ask of the narrator?

10. What does the narrator decide to do at the end of the chapter?

Answers
1. The narrator describes the day at the start of the chapter as clear and bright.
2. The short-order cook assumes that the narrator would like a pork chop.
3. The blueprint man asks the narrator if he has the dog.
4. The narrator sees a copy of *Totem and Taboo* (by Sigmund Freud) open in the office.
5. Based on their plush office, the narrator decides that the men who operate this firm are extremely powerful. He calls them "Kings of the Earth."
6. The narrator's mind whirls when the man asks him if he has ever considered switching to another college.
7. In the midst of talking with the man, the narrator remembers the words of advice that his grandfather once told him.
8. The man the narrator is talking with turns out to be Mr. Emerson's son.
9. At the end of their conversation, the man asks the narrator not to tell anyone about the conversation.
10. At the end of the chapter, the narrator decides to call the Liberty Paint company about a job that young Emerson had mentioned.

Suggested Essay Topics
1. The narrator's conversation with Emerson's son has many twists and turns. What happens that complicates the discussion they have? Is it clear that Emerson's son wishes to help the narrator? Why or why not?
2. The narrator thinks very deeply about a song he heard on the subway after leaving Emerson's office. What is the sig-

nificance of the song, both in the chapter and in the novel thus far? Discuss how the story in the song applies to the narrator's life, especially to what Bledsoe has done to him.

Chapter Ten

New Characters:

Mr. MacDuffy: *an inconsequential little man who sends the narrator to work for Mr. Kimbro*

Mr. Kimbro: *a demanding boss who tells the narrator what to do with the paint*

Lucius Brockway: *the man in charge of the boilers; An old black man, Brockway is wise in the workings of both the people and machinery of the paint factory.*

Summary

The narrator goes to a paint factory in Long Island. He uses Emerson's name to get the job, and he is nervous about it. The narrator is sent to Mr. Kimbro, who gives him directions for adding an ingredient to the paint. This begins well, until the narrator draws his mixing material from the wrong tank. This taints the buckets, and incurs Kimbro's wrath. The narrator seems to get another chance, but this only forestalls the inevitable.

The narrator is ready to leave the factory. Instead, he is sent to the boiler room, as a new assistant to Lucius Brockway. The narrator sees that Brockway is an unpleasant boss. Distrustful, sarcastic, and abusive, Brockway does not wish to share his realm or his power. Yet he allows the narrator to stay.

The narrator learns that Brockway is the unofficial chief engineer of the entire factory, manufacturing the foundation of the paint, and is intimately familiar with all of the physical plant.

What the narrator is not aware of, but finds out, is that association with Brockway is dangerous. The young blacks active in the unions condemn Brockway's isolationist position, while Brockway himself is put in a rage to hear that the narrator has had anything

Chapter 10

to do with the union men.

The fight that the narrator and Brockway have over this subject is based on a misunderstanding, yet its violence escalates. Brockway escapes just before the huge explosion that ends the chapter. The narrator is not so fortunate.

Analysis

The narrator begins work feeling that he has made a move of his own to improve his life. Yet he finds that he has taken someone else's job, and benefited from a misunderstanding about his having been to college.

After his initial problems, his move to the boiler room proves to be small improvement. The relationship between Brockway and the other black laborers at the factory provides the narrator with yet another lesson in the politics of race and power.

What Brockway shows the narrator, and the reader, is how he has kept his position and his power. Brockway's career and survival are remarkable. He is perfectly aware of this, as we see in the anecdote about Mr. Sparland, the rich owner, who visited Brockway in person to convince him not to retire.

What has allowed Brockway to succeed, especially in his later years, is a complete conviction in what he does. He has no time to be, or interest in being, ambivalent. This has kept him focused on living his life, which involves a lot of responsibility and self-satisfaction.

Everyone who comes into Brockway's world represents a potential threat, including the narrator. At first, Brockway decides that the narrator is harmless. When that perception changes, then Brockway must act to protect himself, which he does.

Some of the conversation between Brockway and the narrator recalls what the Vet had said in Chapter Three. Both of the men have spent far more time around white people than the narrator has at that point in his life, and they have learned the truths to which the narrator alluded in the Prologue.

Twice in this chapter, the narrator's name is spoken. It represents the first confirmation that he has a name, but does not shed light on why that name is never shared with the reader.

Study Questions

1. How does the narrator describe the paint factory?
2. What apparently embarrassing thing does the office boy call Mr. Kimbro?
3. Where does Kimbro say the paint is destined?
4. How does Lucius Brockway respond to the news that the narrator is to be Brockway's new assistant?
5. What does the narrator do that satisfies Brockway?
6. Who thought up the factory's slogan about the Optic white paint?
7. Why do the men at the union meeting react so negatively to the narrator?
8. How does Brockway react when the narrator tells him about his contact with the union men?
9. Although the narrator believes at first that Brockway had cut him with a knife, what does Brockway actually do?
10. How does the narrator describe Brockway as the latter is running away?

Answers

1. The narrator describes the paint factory as a small city.
2. The office boy calls Mr. Kimbro a "slave-driver," at which Mr. Kimbro turns slightly red.
3. Kimbro tells the narrator that the paint is destined for the national monument.
4. Lucius Brockway responds with dismissive annoyance to the news that the narrator is to be his new assistant.
5. The narrator manages to satisfy Brockway by reading a pressure gauge correctly.
6. Lucius Brockway thought up the slogan "If it's Optic White, it's the Right White." When the narrator hears this slogan quoted, it makes him think about a rhyme from his childhood, one that sounds similar but means something very different.

7. The men at the union meeting react negatively to the narrator because they believe him to be a spy (or "fink") from the management.
8. When he hears that the narrator was briefly detained at a union meeting, Brockway reacts with extreme and unreasonable anger. It transpires that Brockway believes that the union is somehow trying to take his job away.
9. Far from cutting the narrator, Brockway bites him. This causes Brockway's false teeth to fall out.
10. The narrator describes Brockway as looking "like a small boy who has thrown a brick into the air."

Suggested Essay Topics

1. A wide variety of people interact with the narrator at the paint factory. How do they treat him? Follow the action of the chapter, and include some discussion of all of the interactions. Is there racism? Is the narrator treated as an individual?
2. Write a character sketch of Lucius Brockway, given what we are told in this chapter. Beyond this, what inferences can be drawn? Be sure to support your observations.

Chapter Eleven

Summary

This chapter is reminiscent of Chapter Five, in that not much happens. The scene is static, and the action is internal. We gather that the narrator is receiving medical treatment from doctors, as a result of the explosion in the boiler room. Yet what begins as compassion turns first to ambiguousness and then swiftly to frightening malice. The doctors are actually torturing him, and his agony is more than simply physical; the questions they ask him, or he asks himself, concern his origins and identity.

At the end of the "medical treatment," the narrator is not

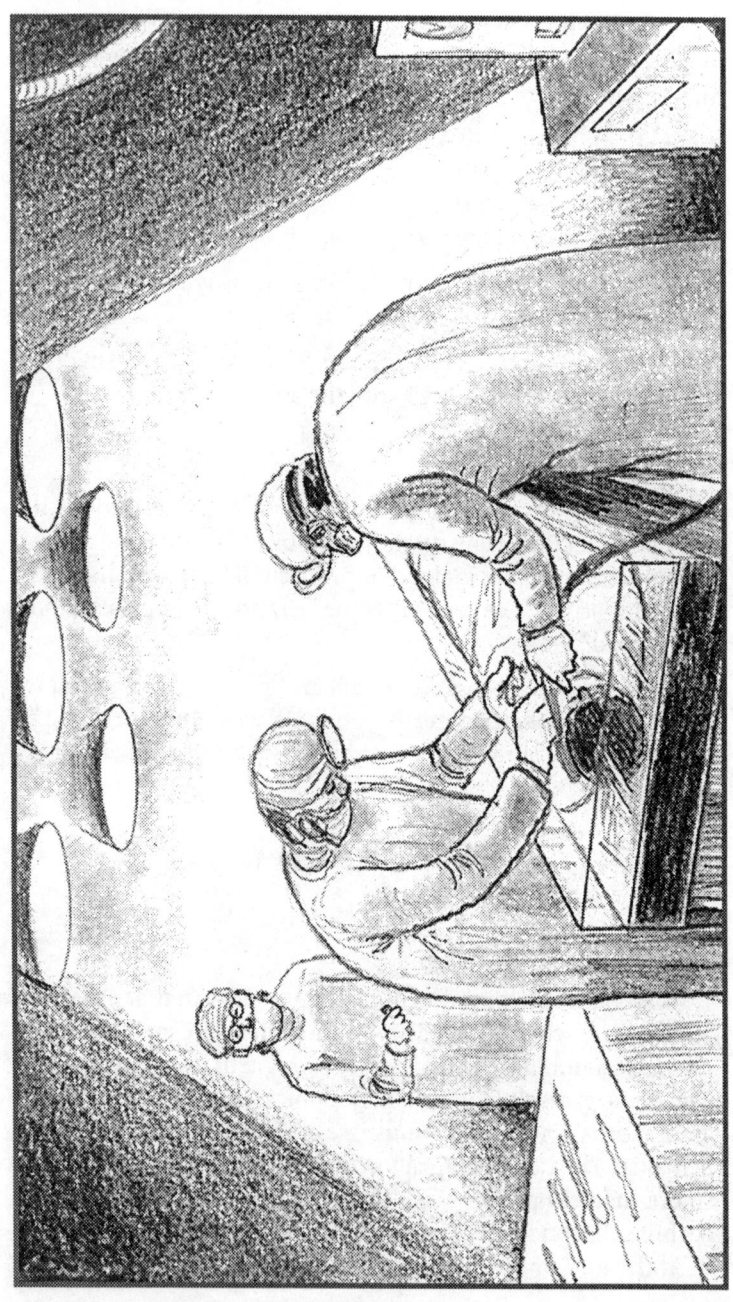

Chapter 11

completely lucid. After more conversation, during which he asks nonsense questions, he leaves. He shows little awareness of his surroundings.

Analysis

If any one part of the novel suggests the possibility that the narrator is not mentally sound, it is this chapter. The questions of the "doctors," and the thoughts that those questions provoke, clearly show the deep confusion inside the narrator. This confusion manifests itself toward the end of the chapter, in both the questions he asks and the descriptions of the world around him.

One possibility to consider is that, in addition to his recent accident at the factory, the narrator is probably very tired. The incident at Jim Trueblood's cabin took place not many months before, and in that time the narrator has had a lot of exhausting adventures.

Study Questions

1. Do the people around the narrator tell him where he is or what has happened to him?
2. What piece of music is formed by the sounds the narrator hears in the beginning of the chapter?
3. What is the first actual "treatment" the narrator receives in the chapter?
4. Is the narrator lying on an operating table?
5. What childhood song does the narrator remember one of his grandparents singing to him?
6. What is the first of the written questions the author is asked?
7. What does the narrator realize regarding the first question?
8. When he is finally released, what is the narrator told?
9. Whom does the narrator ask the doctor if he knows?
10. What form of transportation does the narrator use at the end of the chapter?

Answers

1. No, the people around the narrator do not tell him where he is or what happened to him.

2. The sounds the narrator hears form the opening motif of Beethoven's Fifth Symphony.

3. The first actual "treatment," if that is an appropriate word for it, that the narrator receives in the chapter takes the form of electric shocks. They are repeated later.

4. No, the narrator is not lying on an operating table. He realizes that he is inside a glass-and-metal box.

5. The narrator remembers a little rhyme that his grandmother sang to him.

6. The first of the written questions the narrator is asked is, "What is your name?"

7. Regarding that first question, the narrator realizes that he has forgotten his name.

8. When he is finally released, the narrator is told that he will be compensated for his accident, but that he must now look elsewhere for (less physically demanding) work.

9. The narrator asks the doctor if the latter knows Mr. Norton and "Bled," meaning Dr. Bledsoe.

10. At the end of the chapter, the narrator uses a subway.

Suggested Essay Topics

1. This chapter shows a great range of internal moods in the narrator. Describe when and why his mood changes, especially based on the questions and his reactions to them.

2. How do the doctors and nurses treat the narrator, both in terms of what they do and how they do it? How does the behavior of these people compare to the treatment that the narrator has received from whites in the past?

Chapter Twelve

New Character:

Mary (Mary Rambo) (Miss Mary): *the woman who finds the narrator on the street and brings him to her home.*

Summary

Having left the place where he spent Chapter Eleven, the narrator is very disoriented. After fainting in the street, he is found by Mary Rambo, who insists that he comes home with her to recuperate from his troubles. After a long sleep, he feels better. Although reluctant at first, the narrator decides to accept Mary's offer of low rent, especially once he realizes that the Men's House is not a home.

Believing that he sees Bledsoe, the narrator commits a serious faux pas by dumping something (probably a spittoon) on the head of a Baptist preacher.

As he settles into his new home, the narrator is aware of new feelings of intense anger inside him.

Analysis

This chapter contains the first act of kindness in the novel, and the first period of rest for the narrator. Though the narrator regains the equilibrium he lost in the previous chapter, he feels that he has lost his direction. At the same time, he discovers new feelings deep inside himself; we can tell that he is still learning about himself. This is an important time for the narrator.

The narrator's comprehensive description of the residents of the Men's House contains many observations he had not made earlier, and highlights his growing ability to notice.

Study Questions

1. Does the narrator attract much attention when he faints in the street?
2. How does Mary know that the narrator had been in a hospital?
3. What does Mary give the narrator to eat?

Chapter 12

4. What does the narrator say when Mary asks him what he plans to make of himself?
5. What does Mary say the narrator should not do?
6. Does Mary tell the narrator to stay away in the future?
7. What impression does the narrator get when he goes back to the Men's House?
8. What does the narrator do after dumping something on the wrong man?
9. What is the consequence of what the narrator had done?
10. How does the narrator describe the new emotion that he begins to recognize in himself at the end of the chapter?

Answers

1. Yes, the narrator does attract a crowd when he faints in the street.
2. Mary knows that the narrator has been in a hospital because she smelled ether in his clothes.
3. Mary gives the narrator a cup of hot soup to eat.
4. The narrator says that he had planned to be an educator, but that now he doesn't know.
5. Mary says that the narrator should not forget the struggle, or become corrupted.
6. No, Mary does not tell the narrator to stay away in the future. On the contrary, she tells him that he is welcome to rent a room at her home.
7. The impression that the narrator gets when he goes back to the Men's House was one of alienation and hostility. He feels that he is unwelcome there.
8. Upon dumping what was probably a spittoon on the man whom he felt sure was Bledsoe, the narrator ran out of the Men's House before anyone could stop him.
9. The consequence of the narrator's act is that he is barred

from the Men's House for "ninety-nine years and a day."

10. The narrator describes his new feelings of intense anger as the melting of long-frozen ice.

Suggested Essay Topics

1. Describe Mary. What does the reader know about her, and what does the advice that Mary gives the narrator tell us about her?

2. The narrator sees many different kinds of people when he goes back to the Men's House. His descriptions of the men reveal a lot about how they live in Harlem. What does the information in each of the brief descriptions tell us about the men?

Chapter Thirteen

New Character:

Brother Jack: *the first member of the Brotherhood, a group the narrator becomes involved with*

Summary

While walking the streets, the narrator finds a man selling yams (sweet potatoes) from a cart. The moment the narrator bites into one, he feels homesick. Yet he also feels far better than he had before, and he returns to buy two more yams. Immediately afterward, the narrator becomes involved in a dispute when he sees the eviction of an old black couple. To avoid violence, the narrator gives an impromptu speech, which has a great impact on the crowd. When many police arrive, and a riot looks imminent, the narrator escapes with the help of a white girl.

Soon afterward, a man approaches the narrator and suggests that they talk. Although quite suspicious, the narrator meets with Brother Jack, as the man calls himself. The narrator learns that the movement is interested in universal brotherhood, yet the narrator

Chapter 13

himself is not at all sure that he shares this point of view—his loyalties are determined by race.

The narrator is left to consider his options.

Analysis

The narrator shows more emotion, especially positive emotion, in this chapter. Having endured many misfortunes, he is learning more and more about himself. He feels a new vitality when he pursues what he cares about—foods that he enjoys eating, and public speaking, a subject with which the narrator has had several important experiences.

The narrator spoke to avoid violence, and was able to speak movingly because he cared deeply about his subject. The narrator's success in public speaking reaches back to the first chapter; it is the one subject where his natural talent has been recognized by others. The fact that his talent in this area was immediately recognized opens new doors for the narrator.

Study Questions

1. Where does the yam seller guess the narrator is from?
2. Does the narrator say if he is from that place?
3. What is the crowd doing at the eviction?
4. Of the items the narrator describes coming out of a drawer, which is the oldest and most important?
5. Why does the old woman want to go back into her home for the last time?
6. What does the narrator first say that the people must do?
7. Does the crowd withhold its violence, as the narrator urges them to do?
8. What does the narrator do when police reinforcements arrive?
9. What is the narrator thinkning about when the mysterious white man finds him?
10. What new food does the narrator eat in the cafeteria?

Chapter 13

Answers

1. The yam seller guesses that the narrator is from South Carolina.

2. The narrator does not say whether or not he is from South Carolina.

3. The crowd at the eviction is silently watching the white men, wanting to attack them.

4. Of all the objects the narrator describes coming out of the drawer, the oldest and most important are the "free-papers" of Primus Provo, signed by owner John Samuels in April, 1859.

5. The old woman wants to go back into her home for one last time in order to pray.

6. The narrator first says that the people must organize.

7. No, the crowd does not withhold its violence, as the narrator urges them to do. They charge up the stairs and beat up the policemen.

8. The narrator escapes over the rooftops when the police reinforcements arrive.

9. The narrator is thinking about a baby just being born when the mysterious white man finds him.

10. The narrator eats cheesecake, which he never heard of before, in the cafeteria.

Suggested Essay Topics

1. Discuss the significance of the narrator's experience with the yam seller. How does it compare with the narrator's breakfast in the diner in Chapter Nine? Why does eating the yams make the narrator think and feel about Bledsoe?

2. Summarize the narrator's interview with Brother Jack in the cafeteria. How does each feel about the eviction, and how does each respond to the other's viewpoint? What does the encounter help you learn about each of the characters?

Chapter Fourteen

New Character:

Emma: *an attractive woman involved in the Brotherhood. She lives well and hosts Brother Jack and others for a combination business-meeting/party.*

Summary

Despite some reluctance, the narrator decides to call Brother Jack, who asks the narrator to join him immediately. The narrator meets other members of the Brotherhood, including Emma, the affluent hostess of that evening's meeting.

The narrator is still suspicious and apprehensive, and the reactions from the party members do not relieve these feelings. They talk in a grand manner, and at first almost seem to disregard the narrator's presence. They discuss making him into a great speaker, like Booker T. Washington. They have plans to change his life— a new place to live, new clothes, and even a new name, which Emma gives to the narrator for him to memorize.

Before the narrator can get used to such a barrage of information, he is introduced to a crowd having gathered for a party. There are many important people there, all of whom are eager to talk. Also at the party is a drunk man, who loudly asks that the narrator sing a song. This provokes an angry reaction from Brother Jack, and the drunk man is thrown out. The narrator is amused, yet his reactions are conflicting. After staying at the party for a while longer, the narrator goes home to Mary, wondering about the changes ahead of him.

Analysis

Just as the narrator has shown signs of living a settled life, he becomes involved in a new "adventure." His speech at the eviction led directly to the Brotherhood, and now he has a new job, around white people who are specifically interested in him and what he can do.

Chapter 14

The tense moment regarding the narrator's singing touches on a major theme in this novel: the difficulty of being true to one's self when all those around one make assumptions about one's identity. While it may not be right to assume that all black people enjoy singing, it is also not right to avoid singing merely because people will expect it.

The narrator is frequently worried by the expectations of others. This confuses him and makes him feel ambivalence. The dynamics of the situation with the drunk man are echoed in the narrator's thoughts, in Chapter Thirteen, about eating fried sweet potato pies. He realizes that it is a waste of time to be concerned with what other people expect him to do or say, yet escaping from these feelings is difficult for him.

Study Questions

1. What changes the narrator's mind about calling Brother Jack?
2. What is the name of the expensive-looking building to which Brother Jack takes the narrator?
3. How does the narrator describe the apartment where he meets the other Brotherhood members, including Emma?
4. What drink does the narrator ask for?
5. What does Emma say that offends the narrator?
6. With what was Brother Jack so impressed?
7. Describe the narrator's reaction when Brother Jack suggests that the narrator could be the next Booker T. Washington.
8. To whom does the narrator compare Booker T. Washington?
9. What does Emma challenge the narrator to do?
10. About what does the narrator feel guilty at the end of the chapter?

Answers

1. Literally speaking, the smell of cabbage changes the narrator's mind about calling Brother Jack. In the larger sense, the realization that he needs money changes the narrator's mind regarding whether or not to call Brother Jack.

2. The name of the expensive-looking building to which Brother Jack takes the narrator is Chothian, which means "of the underworld."

3. The narrator describes the apartment where he meets the other Brotherhood members, including Emma, as expensive. It holds many books, musical instruments, and fine furniture. In another room there are lush draperies and a grand piano.

4. The narrator asks for and is given bourbon.

5. The narrator is offended to hear Emma ask whether the narrator should not, ideally, be a little blacker.

6. As he tells the Brotherhood members at Emma's apartment, Brother Jack was very impressed by the narrator's "speech" at the eviction.

7. The narrator's reaction to Brother Jack's idea is one of incredulity, and the narrator looks for humor in Brother Jack's face.

8. The narrator compares Booker T. Washington to the Founder (the man who supposedly founded the college that the narrator attended).

9. Emma challenges the narrator to dance with her, and they dance.

10. At the end of the chapter, the narrator feels guilty about leaving Mary's place. He feels that his decision will seem like ingratitude for her kindness and generosity.

Suggested Essay Topics

1. Examine the narrator's reactions to the drunk man who asks him to sing. How does the narrator respond? Why does he respond in this way, and why does his response get such a reaction from those around him?

2. What does the reader know about the Brotherhood thus far? Review what Brother Jack says in chapter thirteen, combined with relevant quotations and material in this chapter, and sum up the group's philosophy and agenda.

Chapter Fifteen

Summary

The narrator wakes up on his last morning in Mary's place. It is a cold morning, and the heat has gone out. Other tenants of the building protest by banging on the pipes, and this enrages the narrator. He grabs a ceramic "piggy bank" shaped like a caricatured black man and smashes it against the pipes. It shatters, and the narrator feels guilty. He resolves to take the mess away with him and throw it out, regardless of the money.

The narrator joins Mary for a brief breakfast. He gives her a hundred-dollar bill, which she nervously accepts. A horde of roaches comes out of the floor, and Mary and the narrator smash them with their feet and a broom. Once on the street, the narrator drops the package in a garbage can, but is instantly commanded to take it back. The woman of the house lectures him on bad manners and will not listen to his reasonable appeals. He soils his arm in retrieving the package. Next he leaves it on the sidewalk, yet a man follows him for two blocks to give it back to him, amid ludicrous accusations that the narrator was trying to plant incriminating evidence of some kind.

The narrator's mood turns as he buys the clothes that Brother Jack demanded. The narrator sees an article on the eviction protest, which refers to him in passing. After selecting his new clothes, the narrator finds his new address.

Analysis

This chapter is filled with symbols of the narrator's change, from Mary's friend to whatever role the Brotherhood has in store for him. The little home he had with Mary turns from cosy to grimy on his last morning. Not only does everything go wrong, but much of what happens is full of significance.

First of all, the narrator smashes a representation of the old black man, an object he had lived with but never noticed. Next, in the midst of his guilt about abandoning the life he had at Mary's, the roaches make their appearance.

Upon leaving Mary's apartment, the narrator has great difficulty in discarding the package of coins and smashed ceramic. Local black people remind him of his burden and refuse to let him hide it from view, as would be convenient for him.

Having made a real life for himself with Mary, the narrator is trying to change into something else. The world sends its little comments on this day, much like certain catastrophes are interpreted as signs of a god's displeasure. While this may seem an overly dramatic reading, consider all of the odd details of the chapter, in which the narrator is faced with yet another shift in identity.

Study Questions

1. What noises awaken the narrator at the start of the chapter?
2. What are Mary's feelings about the pipe-banging?
3. When Mary assumes that the narrator wants to apologize about unpaid rent, what does she say about it?
4. Where does Mary assume that the narrator got the money he gives her?
5. What does the unpleasant woman threaten to do when the narrator leaves his package in her garbage can?
6. For what two reasons does the man bring the narrator his package?
7. What was the narrator called in the newspaper article about the eviction protest?
8. How is the narrator greeted when he finds his new address?
9. What is the narrator's reaction to his new home?
10. What does the narrator mention is still in his briefcase?

Answers

1. At the start of the chapter, the narrator is awakened by the sounds of his alarm-clock and by the din of tenants hammering on pipes.
2. Mary's reaction to the pipe-noises is that the tenants should know by now that the heat goes out when the landlord is sleeping drunk, or looking for his woman, so that knocking the pipes serves no purpose.

3. When Mary assumes that the narrator wants to apologize about unpaid rent, she says she does not want the narrator worrying, because there will be time to pay it when he has a job.
4. Mary assumes that the narrator got his money by playing the numbers.
5. The unpleasant woman threatens to call the police unless the narrator retrieves his package from her garbage can.
6. When the man first stops the narrator in the street, he assumes that the narrator left his package behind by mistake. Then, when the narrator says that he left nothing behind, the man becomes very suspicious and upset, thinking that the narrator was ditching illegal goods.
7. In the newspaper article on the eviction protest, the narrator was called a "rabble-rouser."
8. The narrator is greeted in a very friendly fashion by his new super (superintendent of the building).
9. The narrator's reaction to his new home is that while it is much more room than he needs, it is clean and neat, and he likes it immediately.
10. At the end of the chapter, the narrator mentions that the broken bank is still in his briefcase.

Suggested Essay Topics

1. Discuss the narrator's thinking about leaving Mary's place and going to the address the Brotherhood has found for him. Why does he think that it might be a bad idea? What advantages are there to moving? How does he explain his decision to himself?
2. What reasons do the woman and the man give for not wanting anything to do with the narrator's package? Is what they say motivated from bitterness, or anger, or other emotions? Also, how does the narrator respond in each of the conversations?

Chapter Sixteen

New Character:

Brother Wrestrum: *the chief speaker of the Brothers present when the narrator gives his speech*

Summary

The narrator accompanies Brother Jack and other Brotherhood members to the rally mentioned at the end of the previous chapter. When they arrive, the narrator is instructed to pay close attention to the other speakers, as the narrator himself will be speaking last.

The rally takes place in a sports arena, and the narrator notices the picture of a well-known boxer. The narrator is reminded of the stories about this boxer, whose career ended in a scandalous fight that left him blind. The narrator then begins to think about the person he is becoming, in his new suit and new name. He ponders whether or not he knows this new person.

One set of thoughts leads to the next, until the Brotherhood group finally enters the arena. The narrator stumbles while walking, but then regains his balance. The speeches blend into each other, without making much impression on the narrator, until it is his turn to speak.

Although the narrator feels he started off badly, his ability to move a crowd comes to him, and he finishes amid the roars of the audience. Moments after the congratulations of the crowd, some members of the Brotherhood severely criticize the narrator's performance, using forms of disapproval from "unsatisfactory" to "hysterical." Although there is division on whether or not the speech was damaging, it is decided that the narrator will study with Brother Hambro and be trained to "speak scientifically."

The narrator goes home and broods on the evening. Memories of his grandfather recur, as do memories of Woodbridge, an English professor from college. This thought leads to Bledsoe and Norton, and the harm that they did to the narrator. The narrator resolves to learn from Hambro and then be done with him, the better to do his own work.

Chapter 16

Analysis

Despite the catty remarks in Emma's apartment, this chapter holds the first real indications of reversals and instability that the narrator faces in the Brotherhood. After a seemingly powerful and certainly successful speech, the narrator is confronted with disgust and disdain from certain members of the organization.

Added to this is the narrator's recurrent questions about identity. While waiting to go into the arena, he asks himself about the person he is becoming. After the speech, when the narrator has time to reflect on both the speech itself and on the different receptions it received, he again wonders about what is real, in his life and within his personality. This vulnerability will not serve him well in surroundings that are already unpredictable.

Notice that one image early in the chapter is significant—that of the boxer who was beaten into blindness. Moreover, references to blindness show up in the narrator's speech. The question of sightlessness is linked to invisibility, since boxers generally fight for the profit and entertainment of others and are less likely to be perceived as true individuals. Also, it is hard to avoid invisibility when one cannot even see both one's self or the people around one.

Study Questions

1. How long does Brother Jack say they will wait before entering the main hall?
2. How did the narrator hear about the boxer and his blindness?
3. Of what does Brother Jack remind the narrator?
4. What members of the audience make the narrator apprehensive?
5. How does the narrator describe Brother Jack as a speaker?
6. What makes the narrator feel that he can begin his speech on a good footing?
7. How does the crowd respond when the narrator's speech is over?

Chapter 16

8. What do the Brothers (led by Brother Wrestrum) claim they have that the narrator does not have?
9. What conclusion do the Brothers reach regarding the narrator's future as a speaker for the Brotherhood?
10. What is Brother Jacks's reaction to what the Brothers say about the narrator's speech?

Answers

1. Brother Jack says they will stay out of the main hall until the crowd has reached the height of their impatience.
2. The narrator's father had told the narrator about the boxer and his blindness.
3. The narrator realizes that Brother Jack reminds him of Master, a bulldog the narrator knew when he was a child.
4. The policemen in the audience make the narrator apprehensive, until Brother Jack tells him that they are there to protect the speakers.
5. The narrator describes Brother Jack as "dignified and benign, like a bemused father listening to the performances of his children."
6. The narrator feels he can begin his speech on firm footing when the audience responds to him. First the crowd is patient with him with the microphone, and then someone encourages him. The narrator feels he has made a contact.
7. The narrator describes the audience's reaction as being "like a clap of thunder," with the crowd shouting, cheering, and whistling.
8. The Brothers (led by Brother Wrestrum) claim they have a scientific approach to society, which the narrator lacks. This is what made his speech so "damaging."
9. Regarding his future as a speaker for the Brotherhood, the Brothers conclude that the narrator must study under Brother Hambro, who will train the narrator to speak more appropriately.

10. Brother Jack responds first with angry sarcasm to the reactions of the other Brothers. Soon afterward, he is more accepting of their position.

Suggested Essay Topics

1. Go through the chapter and compare all the moments where the narrator mentions sight in one way or another. The discussion of this chapter includes some comments on blindness, and the narrator makes many other references to being seen, the uses of sight, and the forms of blindness. Explain his references to what eyes do or cannot do, in both the narration and the quotations, in terms of the novel thus far.

2. Discuss Brother Jack's reactions to the narrator's speech and to what the other Brotherhood members have to say about the speech. What do these reactions reveal about the character? Are they surprising, given what the reader has learned about Brother Jack previously?

Chapter Seventeen

New Characters:

Brother Tarp: *an older man who works at the Harlem Brotherhood office*

Brother Tod Clifton: *another member of the Brotherhood's Harlem office, a charismatic young man*

Summary

Four months have passed, during which the narrator has studied rigorously with Brother Hambro. The narrator and Brother Jack go to a bar in Harlem, where the narrator learns that he is the new chief spokesman for the Brotherhood's Harlem office. Brother Jack cautions the narrator about the uses and misuses of what he has learned. Then the two go to the Harlem office, where they meet

Brother Tarp. An old, physically disabled man, he shows the narrator his new office.

The next morning, Brother Jack calls a meeting in the Harlem office. Brother Tod Clifton is late; his entrance is understated and somewhat dramatic. The narrator describes him as very black and handsome, with a curiously Anglo-Saxon face.

Brother Clifton tells Brother Jack he was late due to a doctor's appointment. He is bandaged, having fought with Ras the Exhorter and his men. The narrator does not recall the name, yet it turns out that the narrator does remember when he first came to New York City, in Chapter Seven, and saw a man speaking from a ladder. That man was Ras.

Brother Jack reminds them that the Brotherhood is opposed to violence. Then Brother Jack leaves, and discussions on strategy and future activities continue. They compare their efforts to galvanize the people to the work of Marcus Garvey, a political activist from many years before who was deported by the U.S. Government.

The narrator and Brother Clifton are speaking to a youth group when Ras and his men arrive. A street fight ensues. Ras defeats Clifton and is poised over him with a knife. Seeing in Clifton a color-traitor, Ras says that he should kill him. Yet Ras is moved to tears, and the narrator sees that Ras is indeed an exhorter.

Ras says that black pride is sapped by whites, that the dregs of white womanhood are offered up as a reward for the essence and the sweat of black men, and that working for the Brotherhood is a fool's paradise. The narrator is held as if by magic, yet both the narrator and Clifton call Ras crazy. The spell is broken only when Clifton knocks Ras out. Clifton and the narrator leave, discussing Ras further.

The next morning, Brother Tarp gives the narrator a picture of Frederick Douglass. The two converse about the great work being done. The narrator calls community leaders regarding plans to protest evictions and gradually notices that his new Brotherhood name is becoming well known in Harlem.

Analysis

The responsibility that the narrator has been seeking is finally his. Having learned the Brotherhood's platform and ideology, he is ensconced as head of the Harlem office. Yet despite the ways in which black and white people are working together, the narrator's ambivalence remains.

Along with Mary, Brother Clifton is one of the most admirable characters the reader has met. His charisma is reflected in the way the narrator describes him, and even in what Ras says to him. This also seems to be a time when the narrator is acting with the noblest of intentions as well. Yet what both Clifton and the narrator say to Ras may cause us to wonder whether or not either of them are such heroes after all.

One of the most telling moments of the chapter is when the narrator says to Clifton that Ras is crazy, to which Clifton agrees. This epithet of "crazy" is clearly a response based on what a listener is hearing, but does not wish to hear. This has occurred before, in the grandfather's deathbed speech and from Mr. Norton regarding the Vet at the Golden Day. But the narrator himself has never pronounced anyone "crazy" until now. This suggests that the narrator is finally in a position to realize when someone is telling him more truth than he is comfortable with hearing.

Study Questions

1. What is the name of the Harlem bar in which the narrator and Brother Jack have their drinks?
2. What does the narrator answer when Brother Jack asks what he thinks of Brother Hambro as a teacher?
3. How does the narrator respond when Brother Jack tells him that he will be the chief spokesman for the Harlem office?
4. What idea does the narrator have to keep eviction protests important to the Brotherhood's agenda?
5. What does one of the men with Ras call the narrator during the street fight?
6. What does the narrator do to Ras to protect Clifton?
7. What does Ras say that Clifton would have been in Africa?
8. After leaving behind Ras, what does the narrator say he is suddenly very glad that he found?

Chapter 17

9. Of whose voice does the narrator remember echoes when he looks at the picture of Frederick Douglass?
10. What does the narrator remember that he has in common with Frederick Douglass?

Answers

1. The name of the Harlem bar in which the narrator and Brother Jack have their drinks is El Toro.
2. When Brother Jack asks the narrator what the latter thinks of Brother Hambro as a teacher, the narrator says that Brother Hambro pushed him hard, and that he (the narrator) certainly has learned a few things.
3. The narrator had been impatiently waiting for the next phase of his career with the Brotherhood and is surprised and elated.
4. The narrator's idea for keeping eviction protests in the forefront of the Brotherhood's agenda is to enlist the help of community leaders.
5. During the street fight, one of the men calls the narrator an "Uncle Tom," meaning a person who loves his oppressors.
6. To protect Clifton, the narrator hits Ras with a pipe on the man's knife hand.
7. Ras says that, in Africa, Clifton would have been a chief, a black king.
8. After leaving behind Ras, the narrator says that he is suddenly very glad that he has found the Brotherhood.
9. When the narrator looks at the picture of Frederick Douglass, he remembered and shut out the echoes of his grandfather's voice.
10. The narrator remembers that Frederick Douglass came from the South to the North, and changed his name, just as the narrator himself has done.

Suggested Essay Topics

1. What are your impressions of the Brotherhood, based on both this chapter, and what you have learned from earlier chapters? How friendly an organization is it, and what about it (if anything) might make you suspicious?
2. Summarize what Ras says to the narrator and Clifton. What are your reactions to the speech he gives them? How does it fit in with the definition of "exhort"? Why do you think they call him crazy?

Chapter Eighteen

Summary

The narrator finds an anonymous letter on his desk, warning him about "moving too fast," considering that he is now in "a white man's world." Upset, the narrator calls in Brother Tarp. In that moment, the narrator sees his grandfather staring at him from Tarp's face.

Once over that shock, the narrator asks Brother Tarp about the letter and about what others think of him. Tarp says he knows nothing about the letter, and has not heard any negative reports on the narrator. Tarp reminds the narrator about a controversial poster, depicting people brought together in universal Brotherhood, which had been the narrator's idea. Tarp says that while some Brotherhood members were against the idea at first, they are now bragging about it.

Tarp then tells the narrator about how he got his limp. There is nothing physically wrong with his leg, but the trauma from dragging a chain (having escaped from a work-gang for some unnamed crime) stayed with him ever since. Tarp unwraps a package from his pocket, revealing the ankle-link he forced open to escape. Tarp gives the narrator the link he kept for so long.

Tarp leaves, and the narrator decides that the letter was sent to confuse him, and he must stay focused on his work. Yet he wonders who sent the letter.

Chapter 18

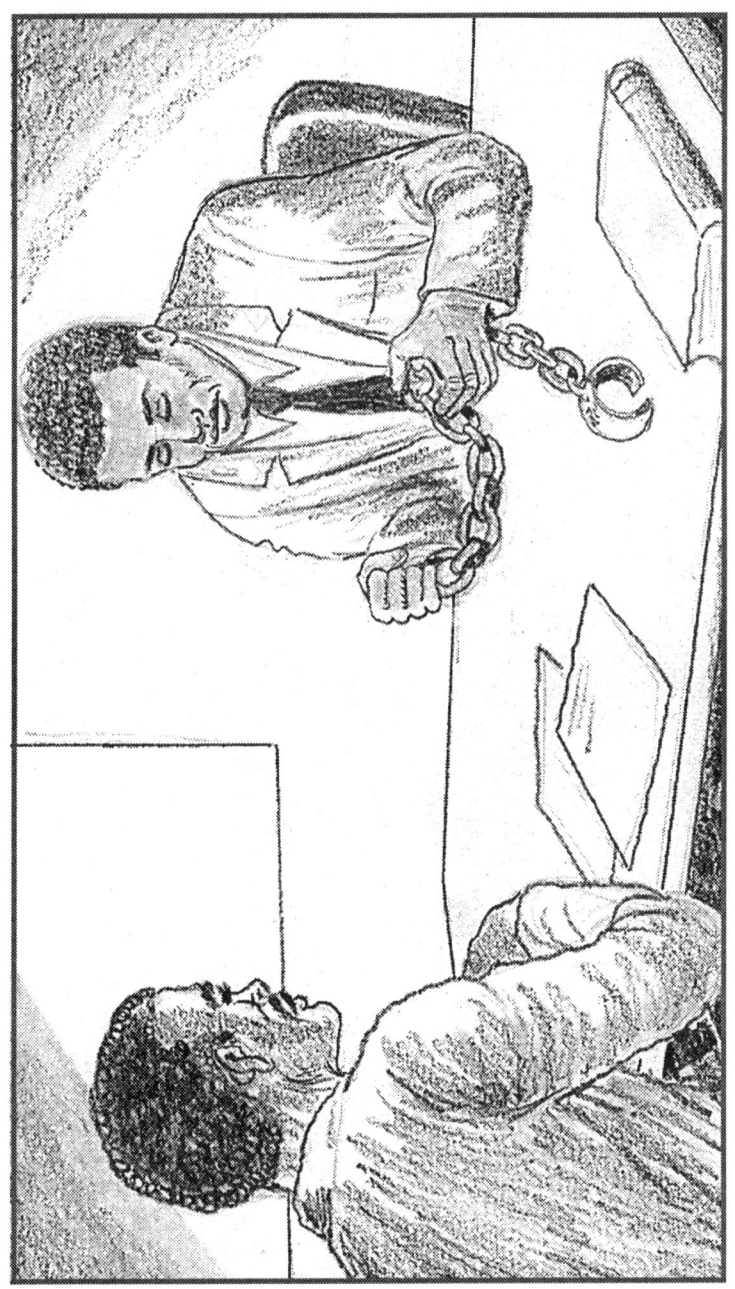

Brother Wrestrum visits the narrator and takes exception to the exposed chain-link. Brother Wrestrum says the Brotherhood has enemies from both without and within. He says he continually questions himself, to make sure that he is serving the Brotherhood properly. That way, he says, Brother Tod Clifton's accident will not be repeated. Clifton was at a rally when a fight began, and he started beating one of the white brothers by mistake.

A magazine editor calls, asking for an interview. The narrator begs off at first, but, as he sees Wrestrum giving his views on what the narrator should do, the narrator decides to give the interview after all. Two weeks later, the narrator goes to a Brotherhood meeting. The agenda begins with charges that the narrator has been guilty of acting to focus attention on himself, rather than serving the Brotherhood selflessly.

Brother Wrestrum shows the brothers a magazine with the narrator's face on the cover with the interview inside . The brothers discuss whether or not the narrator was right to give the interview, and the narrator's position of fame in Harlem. The narrator says he has no need to defend himself, since he was acting in the interests of the Brotherhood.

The narrator is asked to step outside while the committee sifts the information. He is called back and told that no wrong-doing was found. But there are other charges to investigate, and the committee has decided that the narrator is to leave Harlem and take up a new assignment: lecturing on "the woman question". The only alternative is for the narrator to leave the Brotherhood. Overwhelmed by this reversal, where he least expected it, the narrator leaves Harlem quietly, without saying good-bye to his co-workers.

Analysis

This chapter shows more of the Brotherhood's inner workings. Considering that universal cooperation is a tenet of the Brotherhood, the reader finds many instances of misunderstanding and suspicion from most of the brothers. Given what we have seen from other characters, such as the Vet and Emerson's son, these feelings may well be the inevitable result of whites and blacks working together.

Chapter 18

The "hearing" to determine whether or not the narrator acted improperly is a good example of this. Order is lacking, and the cold words increase the strong emotions.

The meeting is different from other confrontations in the novel, in that the narrator is on the same level with his attackers. When facing Bledsoe, or Lucius Brockway, the narrator was younger, a student or worker. Now he is an equal, yet the machinations of others defeat him.

Also significant is Brother Clifton's attack on a white brother. While it is likely that the attack was a mistake, it is also possible that Clifton saw his chance to hit a white man and get away with it. Given what Ras said in the previous chapter, and the reactions his words received, hearing that Clifton attacked a white man may make the reader wonder about Clifton's motives.

Study Questions

1. To whom does the narrator attribute his habit of looking at everything on his desk?
2. Why has the narrator's Brotherhood poster gotten some of the Brotherhood's youth members arrested?
3. How long has Brother Tarp had his limp?
4. According to the narrator's memories, how is Tarp's chain-link different from the one on Bledsoe's desk, back at the college?
5. What is Brother Wrestrum's big idea about which he wants to talk with the narrator?
6. In the committee meeting, what does Brother Wrestrum claim that the narrator wants to become?
7. How does the narrator feel while the committee is discussing Wrestrum's charges?
8. In response to further charges against him, what does the narrator wonder if everyone's been reading?
9. What is the narrator's guide for his new lecture assignment?
10. How did the narrator leave Harlem?

Chapter 18

Answers

1. The narrator attributes his habit of looking at everything on his desk to Bledsoe.
2. Some of the Brotherhood's youth members were arrested for covering up advertisements with the posters, in the subway system.
3. Brother Tarp has had his limp for nineteen years, six months and two days.
4. According to the narrator's memories, the difference between the chain-links is that while Bledsoe's link was smooth, Tarp's link showed "the marks of haste and violence".
5. Brother Wrestrum's big idea that he wants to talk with the narrator about is the need for an emblem, a special pin or button that Brotherhood members can wear and thereby recognize each other.
6. In the committee meeting, Brother Wrestrum claims that the narrator wants to become a dictator.
7. The narrator is "boiling with anger and disgust" as the committee is discussing Wrestrum's charges.
8. In response to further charges against him, the narrator wonders aloud if everyone has been reading a cartoon strip concerned with plots and schemes of evil-doing.
9. The pamphlet "On the Woman Question in the United States," written by Brother Jack, will be the narrator's guide for his new lecture assignment.
10. The narrator left Harlem by simply slipping his papers into his briefcase (the same briefcase he was given at the battle royal). He left as though going downtown to a meeting.

Suggested Essay Topics

1. How do you perceive interpersonal relations at the Brotherhood? What evidence of division can be seen in this chapter? Are these problems of communication simply the standard results of people working together, or are there deep conflicts

between the members of the Brotherhood? Be sure to cite examples and details from the chapter.
2. Describe the meeting in which the narrator faces the charges against him. What is the mood, and how does it change? How do people communicate their views? How does the narrator handle himself? What should he have done differently, and why?

Chapter Nineteen

New Character:

Hubert's wife: *an unnamed woman with whom the narrator has an affair*

Summary

The narrator begins the lectures he was assigned in the previous chapter. He senses that the women, having heard all about him, simply see him before them and are entranced by whatever he says.

At the end of the first lecture, one woman approaches the narrator with a request for further explanations of the Brotherhood's position regarding women. The narrator offers to discuss her questions privately, and she invites him to her apartment. Once there, she explains that her husband, Hubert, is out of town; otherwise, she says, he would have loved to meet the narrator.

It becomes clear to the narrator that the woman's interests are not all intellectual in nature. His feelings are conflicted. He is about to leave when he is overcome by the moment, and he stays.

In the middle of the night, the narrator hears a sound. Looking up from the woman's bed, he sees her husband looking at them. The husband and wife exchange a few brief, pleasant words, and the husband goes off, presumably to sleep in another room.

The narrator, angry with himself, dresses and leaves. The woman has gone back to sleep. The narrator considers whether he was set up in a compromising situation, and waits for words of

Chapter 19

censure and dismissal from the Brotherhood. Nothing happens, and the narrator arranges to meet the woman again. His lecture series continues, and he is more aware of the dynamics between himself and his audiences.

Some time later, the narrator is summoned to a meeting. There, Brother Jack asks the narrator if the latter has seen Brother Tod Clifton. When the narrator says he has not, he is informed of Clifton's disappearance. The narrator is ordered back to Harlem immediately, to find Clifton and to rebuild the Brotherhood's image in the community. The narrator has been gone from Harlem for only one month, but it seems clear that many changes have occurred in that time.

Analysis

As he usually does, the narrator begins a new experience with enthusiasm and energy, without thinking about what misadventures could accompany his actions. Although he claims (in the middle of this chapter's second paragraph) to have a suspicious nature, it does not occur to him that any of the women might be interested in him personally.

The reader can tell that the woman is seducing the narrator not only through what she does, but also by what she says. The first part of the chapter contains many words and phrases that have double meanings. The classic game of flirtation and suggestive language is being played here.

We are given the distinct impression that the woman is white. The narrator's frame of mind, containing anger, excitement, and a little fear echoes the viewing of the naked blond woman in the first chapter's battle royal. The commentary about servants and Pullman attendants trysting with white women also suggest the significance of interracial sexual relationships.

The narrator can see that this extramarital affair is of no importance to the married couple, and this is just a fling of the moment. Yet he elects to see the woman again. He feels off-balance again with his white co-workers, yet the unpleasant surprise at the meeting is not the result of any perceived failure on his part. The narrator remains at the mercy of others.

Study Questions

1. To what famous black actor does the narrator compare himself?
2. How does the narrator describe the woman with whom he discusses ideology?
3. Once inside the woman's spacious apartment, what does the narrator think to himself that he would do if he were really free?
4. From whom does the woman receive a phone call?
5. What does the woman's husband ask his wife to do in the morning?
6. How does the narrator feel when he arranges a second meeting with the woman?
7. Why is the narrator late to the meeting to which he has been summoned?
8. What is Brother Jack's mood on the subject of Brother Clifton's disappearance?
9. Whom does the narrator think might be connected to Clifton's disappearance?
10. What image does the narrator use to describe his mood at the end of the chapter?

Answers

1. The narrator compares himself to Paul Robeson, a famous black actor (and political activist/author) of the 1930s and 1940s.
2. The narrator describes the woman with whom he discusses ideology as "a small, delicately plump woman with raven hair."
3. Once inside the woman's spacious apartment, the narrator thinks to himself that if he were really free, he would leave.
4. The woman receives a phone call from her sister.
5. The woman's husband asks his wife to wake him early in the

morning, because he has a lot of work to do.

6. The narrator feels a "mixture of relief and anxiety" when he arranges a second meeting with the woman.

7. He is late to the meeting to which he has been summoned because he was working on some last minute details regarding his lectures.

8. Brother Jack's mood on the subject of Brother Clifton's disappearance is one of anger and impatience; he says that Ras the Exhorter and his men have taken advantage of the situation to step up their agitation work.

9. The narrator wonders if Ras the Exhorter might be connected to Clifton's disappearance.

10. At the end of the chapter, the narrator says that he feels as though he has awoken from a deep sleep.

Suggested Essay Topics

1. Summarize the narrator's discussion with the woman known only as Hubert's wife. What messages are they sending to each other? Did the narrator have reasonable exepectations for intellectual conversation when he went to her apartment?

2. What is the significance of the husband's appearance in the apartment? What do the narrator and the reader know about the situation that they didn't know before, and how does this knowledge tie in with the conversation between the narrator and the woman?

Chapter Twenty

Summary

The narrator begins searching for both the missing Brother Tod Clifton and Brother Maceo. In the process, the narrator realizes the extent of the damage done to the Brotherhood's reputation and position in Harlem. Stopping in a well-known bar, the narrator finds

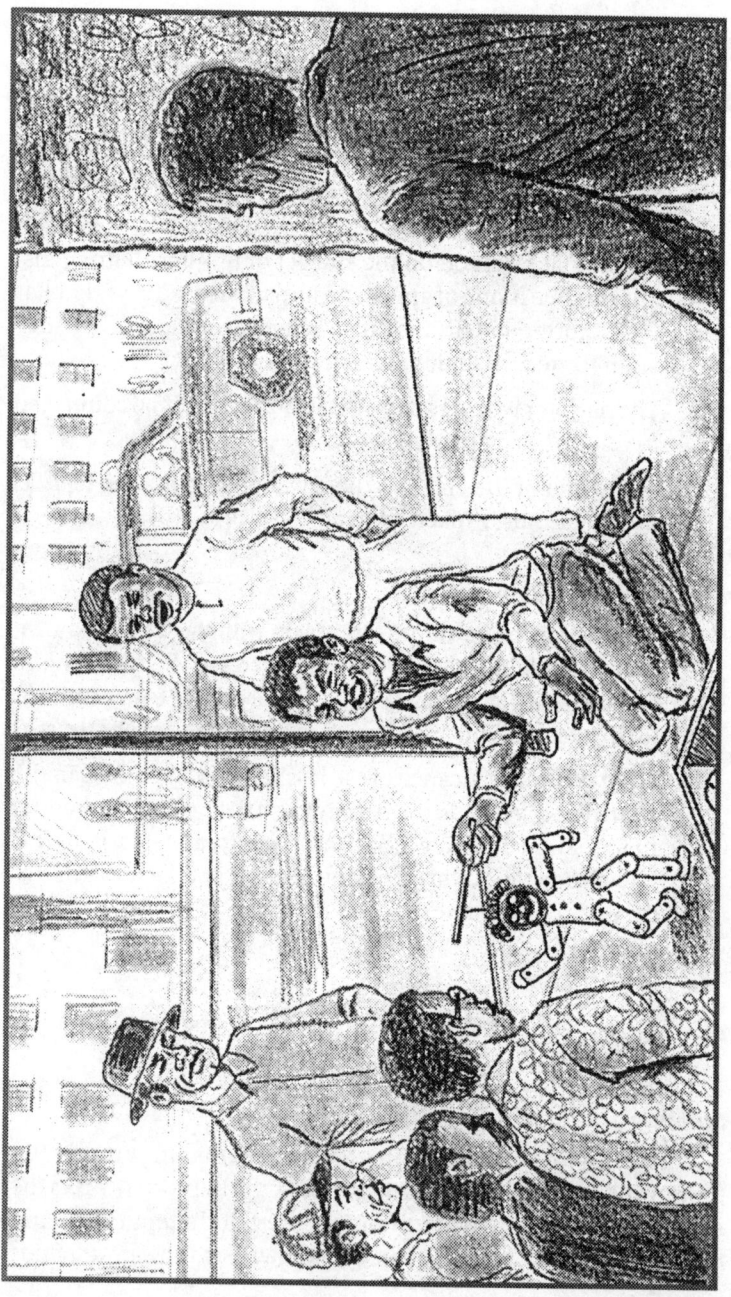

Chapter 20

out how little the Brotherhood is now liked. Only the defense of the friendly bar owner keeps the narrator from an argument with those who decry the Brotherhood, thinking themselves forsaken.

The narrator next tries the Harlem office, to seek out Brother Tarp, who is not there. In the morning, however, a number of Brotherhood members show up. The narrator, in addition to asking about Clifton, hears about the Brotherhood's fall from grace in Harlem.

The narrator needs to confer with the downtown committee. When he is not asked to join their daily meeting, he travels downtown in an effort to ascertain the situation. Shut out and furious, he is on a separate errand when he sees a friend of Clifton's. The narrator is about to ask the man about Clifton when he spies an object in the corner of his vision; it is a Sambo doll, like a marionette. The offensive object is being sold on the street, dancing puppet-style on a flat cardboard square. A sing-song spiel accompanies the pathetic dance, and then the narrator recognizes the man selling the Sambo dolls. It is Clifton.

The narrator, utterly aghast, can hardly believe his eyes. Clifton sees him and smiles awfully, but before the narrator can confront Clifton, the latter vanishes around a corner, running from a policeman. His head swimming with confusion and unanswered questions, the narrator witnesses a short, brutal fight, that ends with Clifton shot by the policeman's gun.

Other police appear, keeping the narrator away from the dead Clifton. There is no one the narrator can talk with, since no one else saw the killing, and the narrator knows of no other friends of Clifton's to seek out. He is trapped with his own thoughts and perceptions, and these shed no light on the situation. The narrator takes to the subways, without a clear destination. He watches the people around him, all strangers.

Analysis

It is hard to reconcile how the Harlem office lost such strength in just a month. The narrator and the reader are in similar positions of wonder and bewilderment.

The latest move from the Brotherhood's central committee is clearly one of exclusion. They have no interest in including the narrator in their meeting, even when the narrator shows up at their headquarters. This can only increase the narrator's paranoia.

The narrator finds Clifton and loses him without first getting any explanation. Selling Sambo dolls in the street seems insane. There is a lot of mystery as to why Clifton fights with the policeman, but the narrator explains it to himself. He thinks about what it is to fall outside of history, as Ras had once talked about. The narrator is finding in this lesson something to grasp and remain true to—the importance of showing history to other people.

Although the story-line remains strong, and has even picked up momentum now, the lack of answers is disturbing, to both the narrator and the reader.

Study Questions

1. What is the name of the bar and grill the narrator visits?
2. What does Barrelhouse say when the narrator asks him how business is going?
3. What reasons does Barrelhouse give for the Brotherhood's fall in popularity?
4. On his way to the Brotherhood's Harlem office, where does the narrator almost go?
5. Why does the narrator expect to find Brother Tarp at the office?
6. Why does the narrator wish to attend the downtown strategy meeting?
7. According to the narrator, when are the strategy meetings generally held?
8. What had the narrator decided to do downtown when he found Brother Clifton?
9. Just before they run around the corner, does Clifton say anything that suggests why the policeman might be after them?
10. What final tribute does Clifton receive from a boy that saw his last fight?

Answers

1. The name of the bar and grill the narrator visits is Barrelhouse's Jolly Dollar.

2. When the narrator asks Barrelhouse how business is going, the latter says that it's really bad, and he doesn't want to talk about it.

3. The reasons that Barrelhouse gives for the Brotherhood's fall in popularity are that there isn't much money in Harlem, and that those who got jobs through the Brotherhood are no longer working.

4. On his way to the Brotherhood's Harlem office, the narrator almost goes to Mary's place.

5. The narrator expects to find Brother Tarp at the office because Tarp sleeps there, or used to. The narrator notes that the room where Tarp slept is empty, with even the bed missing.

6. The narrator wishes to attend the downtown strategy meeting because many of the policies that hurt the Brotherhood's credibility in Harlem seem to issue from the downtown office, and the narrator wanted an explanation.

7. According to the narrator, the downtown strategy meetings are generally held at one o'clock.

8. The narrator decides to shop for a pair of new shoes downtown, just before he sees Brother Clifton.

9. Yes. Just before going around the corner and into an alley, Clifton says something about not having a license for, and therefore not paying taxes on, his Sambo dolls. This suggests that Clifton might not have a permit.

10. The final tribute that Clifton receives is that he sure knew how to use his dukes (fists). The compliment comes from an apple-cheeked little boy who saw Clifton's last fight.

Suggested Essay Topics

1. Describe the mood in Harlem, based on what we read in this chapter. Use specific details from different moments

and incidents, being sure to observe people and descriptions closely, and support your points.
2. Given what we know of Brother Tod Clifton, since having met him, try to give some explanation of his behavior. Concentrate on what Ras said to Clifton and the narrator in Chapter Seventeen. We have seen before that when characters act crazy, or are called crazy, there is generally something more at work. What might that be, in this situation?

Chapter Twenty-One

Summary

The narrator returns to the Harlem district. There are indications that the Brotherhood's position is already improving somewhat, but all the narrator can do is mull over the details of the death and ask himself why he did not do something. He tosses the inert doll on his desk and addresses it bitterly. He then realizes that, distasteful though it might be, a public funeral for Clifton would serve a great purpose.

The youth members, the members of the Brotherhood with whom Clifton had spent the most time, have heard the news and approach the narrator. He confirms the report of Clifton's death. The district begins to respond with organization and anger, and the narrator is kept very busy.

The funeral takes place on a hot Saturday afternoon and draws a great crowd. People from all social circles march, and the police watch carefully. The narrator observes all the details of the spectacle: the cheap gray coffin that seems to float above the heads of the mourners, the people looking on from the streets, the look of the clouds and the birds, and the sound of Tod Clifton's name. Finally, the procession arrives at a local park. There, the narrator is given a signal to begin.

The narrator gives Clifton's funeral address without any prewritten speech or notes. The novel includes all of the speech, which seems to harangue the crowd and sum up all of the

Chapter 21

narrator's weariness and cynicism. As he speaks, the narrator feels that he is not doing it right, that the speech is not political and therefore not useful.

When the narrator is finished, he feels that he has failed. A preacher reads from the Bible, and then the Irish gravediggers bury the casket. The narrator walks the streets, taking in every detail, remaining deeply unhappy.

Analysis

While the narrator is highly aware of the unpleasantness associated with Clifton's death, he also realizes the opportunity for regaining the Brotherhood's lost status in the Harlem district. Whether or not he has forgiven Tod Clifton is not the point any longer.

The community seems to have done the same. Whether or not they have heard how Clifton died, and whether or not they actually came to mourn his death, they did come, and this bodes well for the Brotherhood's position in Harlem.

The narrator took the only constructive approach regarding the funeral, in deciding that the manner of Clifton's death is not nearly as important as what Clifton did as an activist for the Brotherhood. Yet despite this, and despite his anger and eloquence, his speech does not galvanize the crowd in any visible way.

The narrator did not pause to consider (but, given what has happened in his extremely unstable relationship with the Brotherhood's central committee, perhaps should have realized) that giving a speech at Clifton's funeral would make him vulnerable to future accusations and attacks. Not knowing the Brotherhood's position on Clifton, the narrator acts on his personal beliefs.

Study Questions

1. How does the narrator realize how the doll danced?
2. What does the narrator wish he had done to stop Clifton?
3. How do the youth members respond when the narrator tells them that Clifton is dead?
4. What is the name of the park to which the procession travels?
5. What do the black-bordered signs in the procession say?

6. What had a brother in the Parks Department done, to add to the ceremony?
7. To what does the narrator compare the coffin, visible in the procession?
8. What song does the duet of horn and baritone voice sing when the procession arrives at its destination?
9. What is the first question the narrator asks in his funeral address?
10. Whom does the narrator feel would not approve of the speech?

Answers
1. The narrator realizes that the doll dances by use of a nearly invisible black thread attached to the frilled paper of the doll.
2. The narrator wishes he had hit Clifton, gotten into a fight with him. That way, the narrator reasons, Clifton would not have gotten killed.
3. The youth members respond with tears and a desire to go home when the narrator tells them that Clifton is dead.
4. The name of the park to which the procession travels is the Mount Morris Park.
5. The black-bordered signs in the procession say, "BROTHER TOD CLIFTON / OUR HOPE SHOT DOWN".
6. A brother in the Parks Department had opened up one of the towers, and set up sawhorses for the coffin.
7. The narrator compares the coffin to a heavily-loaded ship in a channel.
8. A duet of horn and baritone voice sings "There's Many a Thousand Gone." It moves the crowd greatly.
9. The first question that the narrator asks in his funeral address is "What are you waiting for me to tell you?"
10. The narrator feels that Brother Jack would not have approved of the speech.

Suggested Essay Topics

1. This chapter is filled with questions. Many of them are asked by the narrator, who does not expect an answer. Pick five of the rhetorical questions that the narrator asks and try to provide answers for them, based on what you have read about the subject.

2. Summarize the narrator's funeral address. How many questions does he ask, and of whom does he ask them? What do you think he feels about the audience in the park? Does he say anything about himself, or the Brotherhood? What does he assume, about both Tod Clifton and his audience?

Chapter Twenty-Two

New Character:

Brother Tobitt: *the Brotherhood member who leads the attack upon the narrator in this chapter*

Summary

The narrator goes to the central committee, which is waiting for him. Brother Jack asks about the event, and Brother Tobitt asks why the narrator organized the funeral and the eulogy. The narrator answers reasonably, but emotions escalate immediately.

The committee feels that a traitor such as Clifton did not deserve a hero's burial. But more than this, the committee will not tolerate any member acting alone, as the narrator did. They act as if they concur with Brother Wrestrum's earlier accusation that the narrator is acting selfishly, rather than as part of a machine. The maintenance of discipline is their main focus.

The narrator feels that the situation called for immediate action, rather than for board meetings. The community needed to see that the Brotherhood still cared and was still a presence for change. That could only be accomplished by doing what the narrator did. He operated out of consideration of the community.

Other factors come into play, such as who knows more about the people of Harlem. It transpires that Brother Tobitt is married to a black woman.

The conflict is not easily solved. The parties have no interest in appreciating views other than their own. Since the narrator is outnumbered and without power, he is obliged to acquiesce to the committee's point of view. He is sent to Brother Hambro for further instructions.

Analysis

This chapter contains more sarcasm than any other chapter. The biting and cruel language exposes what the reader may have suspected all along—the realization that there is not very much brotherhood in the Brotherhood.

Brother Jack opens the conversation with what seems to be quiet good humor, but is actually sarcasm in repose. Brother Tobitt's method is almost the same. Their techniques are reminiscent of the narrator's confrontation with Bledsoe in Chapter Six.

The narrator's moods swing somewhat, but he tries hard to keep control of himself. Many themes appear in this chapter: the individual versus the collective, the definition of a traitor, the question of who best knows the people of Harlem (and from where they derived this knowledge), and whether or not complete discipline and sacrifice are worthwhile goals.

Think of this chapter as a play. Much of its action is given in dialogue.

Study Questions

1. Is the narrator surprised to see the committee waiting for him?
2. To whom does Brother Jack compare the narrator, as regards tactical ability?
3. What does Brother Tobitt move that the committee do regarding the narrator's views and remarks?
4. What does Brother Jack remind the narrator that he was not hired to do?

5. With whom does Brother Tobitt say the narrator might be in touch?

6. Midway through the argument with the committee, what does the narrator find and hold tightly in his pocket?

7. Where does Brother Jack put his glass eye the moment it pops out of his head?

8. How does the narrator react to Brother Jack's glass eye coming out of his head?

9. What word does the narrator use to describe Brother Jack's look?

10. What does Brother Jack call the narrator, based on the latter's response to the glass eye?

Answers

1. No, the narrator is not at all surprised to see the committee waiting for him. He is strangely relieved.

2. Brother Jack compares the narrator to Napoleon, when commenting on the former's knowledge of tactics.

3. Brother Tobitt recommends that the committee issue a pamphlet containing the narrator's views and remarks. He is being sarcastic, not sincere.

4. Brother Jack reminds the narrator that he was not hired to think.

5. Brother Tobitt says that the narrator is in touch with God, or at least "the black god." Once again, he is speaking sarcastically.

6. Midway through his argument with the committee, the narrator finds and grips the leg-chain-link from Brother Tarp.

7. The moment Brother Jack's glass eye pops out of his head, he grabs it in midair and plops it into a glass of water.

8. The narrator reacts to Brother Jack's glass eye coming out of his head with shock and disgust.

9. The narrator uses the word "Cyclopean," from the name of

the one-eyed ogre in Greek mythology, to describe Brother Jack's look.
10. Brother Jack, noticing the narrator's response to his glass eye, calls him a "sentimentalist."

Suggested Essay Topics

1. Evaluate the argument from the point of view of your own logic. Whose position in the argument makes the most sense to you? Each stance is well-defined, and thoroughly contradict the other. Be sure to explain which response makes the most sense to you.
2. How do the three men—the narrator, Brother Jack and Brother Tobitt, frame their comments? Which of the comments are sarcastic, and which ones serious? How well does each side communicate with the other?

Chapter Twenty-Three

New Character:

Rinehart: *a shadowy local figure, both a criminal and a preacher, for whom the narrator is repeatedly mistaken*

Brother Maceo: *one of the missing brothers; When the narrator finally finds him, Brother Maceo doesn't recognize him, because the narrator has on his "Rinehart disguise."*

Brother Hambro: *the narrator's "instructor."*

Summary

The narrator goes to Harlem. He avoids conversation, listening instead to the general talk about Clifton's death. Ras is speaking at a streetcorner, from a ladder, and picks out the narrator for special scrutiny. The crowd is sullen, but the narrator defends the Brotherhood and himself, and gets the crowd on his side. Soon afterward, the narrator is attacked by men loyal to Ras and realizes that Ras is becoming bolder.

Chapter 23

Seeing the hipster dress of some men nearby, the narrator ducks into a drugstore and, despite the darkness, gets a pair of sunglasses. The world is different now, and so, it seems, is the narrator. He is immediately mistaken for someone named Rinehart. This happens a total of nine times in the chapter. Wherever the narrator goes, people call him Rinehart or simply assume that he is Rinehart, as long as he wears the dark glasses and the hat he buys. Also, it seems that Rinehart holds many jobs, for police, prostitutes, local toughs, and even church-goers stop the narrator in the street.

The mistaken identity has its advantages, since Ras has continued his rhetoric and is motivating the crowd to vent its anger on whites and members of the Brotherhood. The narrator decides to go to Barrelhouse's bar, where he finds Brother Maceo, whom the narrator had been seeking earlier. Unfortunately, both Maceo and Barrelhouse assume that the narrator is Rinehart, and a simple misunderstanding leads to sudden problems and near-violence.

Finally, the narrator goes to see Hambro, in Manhattan. In response to the narrator's concerns about the Harlem district, Hambro says that the membership must be sacrificed. True to the Brotherhood's rigid adherence to discipline and "scientific objectivity," Hambro agrees that, for the purposes of expediency, those people who have already left the Brotherhood must be considered expendable. According to this view, the committee has a plan that it will announce at the proper time, and there is nothing more to say.

Hambro goes further, saying that it is impossible not to take advantage of the people. The trick was to take advantage of them in their best interests, which would be decided by the committee, using scientific objectivity.

The narrator has heard enough. He leaves and spends the rest of the chapter wrestling with himself. He feels that he has failed the community, that the best he could offer them is the wretched maneuverings of small minds. The narrator resolves to agree with them all, to fool them by acting the fool.

Analysis

The tension in Harlem is mounting steadily. The narrator is becoming more aware of the gulf between the people and the Brotherhood. As if confirming the public's views of the Brotherhood, Brother Hambro's prounouncements about the relationship between the masses and the Brotherhood repulse the narrator. He sees himself as an actor in a play. The Brotherhood's program of utilizing "scientific objectivity" to manage and manipulate people reinforces the Brotherhood's notion that individual people do not matter, as Brother Jack had told the narrator when the two first met. It seems that the Brotherhood is full of people that cannot really see other people for who they are.

That the narrator is mistaken for Rinehart is yet another example of what the narrator comes to believe: that when people look at him, they don't really see him. They simply see what they are expecting to see, whether that's an ignorant southern hayseed, a college boy, a factory worker, a fink, a speech-giver, a criminal, a preacher, or a sexual object. The narrator becomes whatever the observer thinks he or she is seeing.

One of the journeys of this book has been the narrator's realization that not only was his grandfather not crazy, but that what his grandfather said made perfect sense. At the end of the chapter, the narrator is ready for his new course of action.

Study Questions

1. Who aids the narrator when he is set upon by two men loyal to Ras?
2. What color are the lenses of the narrator's dark glasses?
3. In the middle of his sermon against the Brotherhood, what new name does Ras the Exhorter take?
4. What does Barrelhouse call the narrator, thinking him to be Rinehart?
5. Why is Brother Maceo so ready to fight the narrator?

Chapter 23

6. How does one woman recognize that the narrator is not Rinehart (or, as she calls him, Rine the Runner) after all?
7. Where is Rinehart really from, according to one of the old church sisters?
8. What does Brother Hambro say his son is doing?
9. What does the narrator almost forget at Brother Hambro's?
10. Other than deciding to use his grandfather's tactics, what method does the narrator plan to use to get information?

Answers

1. The doorman at a movie theater aids the narrator when the latter is set upon by two men loyal to Ras.
2. The lenses of the narrator's new, dark glasses are a very dark green.
3. In the middle of his sermon against the Brotherhood, Ras the Exhorter changes his name to Ras the Destroyer.
4. Thinking the narrator to be Rinehart, Barrelhouse calls him "Poppa-stopper."
5. Brother Maceo is ready to fight the narrator because he thinks that he is Rinehart, and that Rinehart is about to pull a knife on him.
6. One woman recognizes that the narrator is not Rinehart, or Rine the Runner, by the narrator's shoes, which are not the knob-toed shoes that Rinehart is known to wear.
7. According to one of the old church sisters, Rinehart is from Virginia.
8. Brother Hambro says that his son is wasting time with fancy speeches against going to bed.
9. The narrator almost forgets his hat at Brother Hambro's.
10. Other than deciding to use his grandfather's tactics, the narrator plans to seduce some woman inside or connected with the Brotherhood, in order to acquire more information.

Suggested Essay Topics

1. What do you think about the narrator's reactions to the Brotherhood in this chapter? Brother Hambro has given his thoughts on the organization's decisions and policies, and you have material from other chapters on which to draw. Do the Brotherhood's plans make sense? Why or why not?
2. What is the narrator's response to Rinehart and the roles that Rinehart plays? Summarize the narrator's thoughts on Rinehart.

Chapter Twenty-Four

New Character:

Sybil: *the wife of one of the men (George) in the organization. She and the narrator have an abortive affair*

Summary

The narrator begins to agree with whatever he hears at the Brotherhood, recognizing what it is that the committee wishes to hear and telling them nothing but that. He planned to seduce the wife of one of the Brotherhood's men, and Brother Jack's birthday party is the perfect place for the narrator to select a woman. But the narrator finds that his efforts with Sybil only depress him.

She is interested only in fantasies born out of racism. The narrator seems menacing to the white woman, and Sybil finds this prospect highly titillating. She sees the narrator as a form of entertainment, \and longs to satisfy her assumption that his sexual prowess is far greater than her husband's. Having gotten tipsy, she wants the narrator to rape her, and this disgusts him. Yet he must endure Sybil's inanities when she becomes too intoxicated to leave, and his questions about the Brotherhood lead nowhere. Only a phone call urging the narrator to get up to Harlem ends their tryst.

The narrator puts Sybil in a cab. As he says good-bye, the narrator learns that she does not know his name. A few moments later,

Chapter 24

Sybil appears in the same cab. The narrator has to get rid of her again. Soon afterward, the narrator finds her waiting for him at 110th Street. The narrator puts Sybil in yet another cab and learns that Harlem is being torn apart. He asks her what the leaders of the Brotherhood have planned for him, but gets no answer.

The narrator takes a bus to 125th Street, upset and lost in his own thoughts. He has to use his briefcase as a shield against the pigeon droppings from the birds underneath a bridge.

Analysis

The narrator's unpleasant fling with Sybil occupies most of the chapter. The two characters are acting at cross-purposes, each wanting something that the other cannot provide. Sybil acts very insensitively, but without meaning to, because it never occurs to her that she is treating the narrator as less than a person. For the first time in his life, the narrator decides, or realizes, that he is truly invisible. Sybil sees a black skin, not the person inside of it. This tires and angers him, yet never does he consider doing her any harm, or even trying to reason with her. The narrator is too smart for that.

The violence in Harlem that the narrator has been predicting seems to have arrived. Whether or not the Brotherhood is involved (and it seems unlikely), the climax of the novel is approaching.

Study Questions

1. What does the narrator notice about life in Harlem?
2. Why does the narrator decide not to approach Emma?
3. When Sybil fantasizes about the narrator, whom does she put in his place, mentally speaking?
4. What is Sybil's favorite word for the narrator?
5. What does Sybil tell the narrator she thinks she is?
6. What does the narrator write on Sybil's belly?
7. Does the narrator succeed in making Sybil think he raped her?
8. What is the first thing the narrator wonders when he gets the phone call from Harlem?

9. What does Sybil call the narrator just before she leaves for the last time, and how does he respond?
10. What reason does the narrator give for taking the bus to Harlem?

Answers

1. The narrator notices that Harlem is, as he puts it, "coming apart at the seams." He describes crowds and violence.
2. The narrator decides not to approach Emma because, even if she would sleep with him, she would hardly be likely to give him any information about the Brotherhood.
3. When Sybil fantasizes about the narrator, she puts Joe Louis and Paul Robeson in the narrator's place.
4. Sybil's favorite word for the narrator is "boo'ful," which is short for "beautiful."
5. Sybil tells the narrator she thinks she is a nymphomaniac.
6. The narrator writes "SYBIL, YOU WERE RAPED BY SANTA CLAUS SURPRISE" on Sybil's belly.
7. Yes, the narrator succeeds in making Sybil think that he raped her, by pretending that he does not know her name.
8. The first thing the narrator wonders when he gets the phone call from Harlem is whether it is a trick.
9. Just before leaving the narrator for the last time, Sybil calls him an "ole dictator," to which the narrator responds "a game stud, a most game stud."
10. The reason the narrator gives himself for taking the bus for Harlem is that if Sybil looks for him again, she will not find him.

Suggested Essay Topics

1. The narrator seems to have conflicting emotions in his tryst with Sybil. Explain why this might be the case. What do they say to each other, and what disparate agendas are they pursuing?

2. Write a character summary of Sybil. Why is she in bed with the narrator? What does she want from him? Analyze what she does and what she says.

Chapter Twenty-Five

New Characters:

Dupre: *the leader of a bunch of looters whom the narrator meets during the riots in this chapter*

Scofield: *one of the looters in the group*

Summary

A full-fledged riot takes place in Harlem. Police shoot and the narrator is injured. Stunned, he wipes the blood from his head and continues. He joins a group of looters stealing goods but not harming anyone. They take clothes and various items; the narrator takes nothing, acting only as an observer. The narrator stays near Scofield, who checks the narrator's wound and offers him a drink of scotch.

The narrator feels sure that the riot started because of Clifton's death, but various accounts of its origin are circulating. There is widespread violence, blazing fires, and the unpredictability common to such situations.

A storeowner frantically persuades looters that he is colored, and his store is left undisturbed. At a hardware store, the men take flashlights and full buckets of fuel oil. Moving down the street, they pause at the spectacle of a milk truck topped with a singing fat lady offering free beer. They find this somewhat repellent.

Stopping at a tenement, the narrator sees that the oil was brought to burn it down. Dupre orders the men to evacuate the building. The narrator does not consider protesting, but a young pregnant woman begs Dupre to relent. He refuses.

The men douse the rooms, light their matches, and run down the stairs. The narrator, excited and impressed with the vision and execution of the intention, almost leaves his briefcase behind.

Chapter 25

He is suddenly put in danger when someone calls him by his Brotherhood name. Ras is searching for him, and the narrator slips into the crowd. Soon afterward, more police arrive and are battered by bricks thrown from the rooftops. The riot worsens and gets bloodier.

The narrator runs through the streets and sees more turmoil. He grows steadily angrier at the Brotherhood for having offered false promises for so long.

When he faces Ras and his men, the narrator is exhausted yet determined. He feels that Jack, the committee, and all the white powers in general, are playing some game, and that he is one of the pieces moved across the board of Harlem. The narrator knows that he faces death if Ras gets him, and that the Brotherhood might find this to be very convenient.

However, Ras, now Ras the Destroyer, is acting like some kind of chieftain. He appears on horseback, dressed outlandishly. He throws a spear at the narrator. The narrator rolls clear of the weapon and tries to reason with Ras. When this fails, the narrator is ready to die, but instead takes the spear he has wrenched free and throws it at Ras, piercing both of Ras' cheeks.

The narrator flees, trying to reach Mary's. A broken water main knocks him down, compounding his weariness. He questions his perceptions, feeling unsure of reality. The narrator eavesdrops on two men discussing Ras' battles with the police.

Leaving them, the narrator is accosted by two white men who ask him about his briefcase. Strangely embarrassed, the narrator runs away, and, lifting a manhole cover, drops down into a new darkness. He hears them talk high above and taunts them with words that seem to make no sense.

To see his surroundings, the narrator opens his briefcase and burns what papers he finds there. In the process, he learns that Jack had written the anonymous letter the narrator received in Chapter Eighteen. The shock stupefies the narrator, and makes him scream, and he is soon plunged into fantasies in which Jack, Bledsoe, and others ask him tormenting questions.

When the narrator awakens from this state, he is the narrator of the Prologue, telling the story of his invisibility, which is the story of his life.

Analysis

The landscape of Harlem is analogous to the narrator's inner turmoil. Several things have been coming apart: the Harlem community, the narrator's relationship with the Brotherhood, and his ability to relate to other people.

The scene is completely chaotic, but different from the chaos in the Golden Day, which was jovial and playful. Except for Mr. Norton, there were no whites there to regulate anyone's behavior. Here, the mood is deadly, and police are everywhere. How the riot started is unimportant, except for the fact that the Brotherhood never "saved" the community, as the narrator had once envisioned.

It seems clear that the people of Harlem needed something in which to put their faith, and since the Brotherhood abandoned that role, they turned to violence, which helped Ras.

The people show different responses to Ras. The language that the two men discussing Ras use in their stories is vivid. They condemn his affected "King of Africa" attitude, but they are impressed with the power of his presentation.

The narrator's sense of self and grasp on reality is slipping, or has slipped, away.

Study Questions

1. To what does the narrator compare the sounds he hears when he arrives in Harlem?
2. Why does Scofield assume that the narrator also picked up some "loot"?
3. How does Dupre carry the items taken in looting?
4. What reason does Scofield give for how the riot started?
5. What does Dupre take from his boot to show his serious intention regarding the building?
6. What does Scofield say will be a surprise in the fire?
7. What medical treatment does the narrator render in the street?
8. When the narrator finds him, what is Ras telling the people to do?

9. Once inside the sewer system, what does the narrator tell the men he has in his briefcase?
10. At the end of the chapter, to where does the narrator realize he cannot return?

Answers

1. The narrator compares the sounds he hears when he arrives in Harlem to the Fourth of July.
2. Scofield assumes that the narrator also picked up some loot because of the narrator's briefcase, which is heavy with the smashed ceramic bank from Mary's place.
3. Dupre carries the items he takes in his looting in a huge cotton sack he brought with him from the South.
4. The reason that Scofield gives for the riot is that a policeman slapped a kid for stealing a candy bar, and then slapped the kid's mother.
5. To show his serious intention regarding the building, Dupre takes a nickel-plated revolver from his boot.
6. Scofield says that the bedbugs in his bed will be getting a surprise in the fire.
7. The narrator tightens the tourniquet of a seriously bleeding man in the street.
8. When the narrator finds him, Ras is telling the people to leave off from their looting and to join him in storming the armory for guns and ammunition.
9. Once inside the sewer system, the narrator tells the men on the street that he has them in his briefcase.
10. At the end of the chapter, the narrator realizes that he cannot return to Mary's, or the Brotherhood, or his old campus, or to any part of his former life.

Suggested Essay Topics

1. Is the Brotherhood responsible for the riot in Harlem? Could

the members have prevented it, or was it inevitable? Why does the narrator feel that the Brotherhood should be held accountable for what has happened?

2. When was it clear that the narrator wanted to go to Mary's place? Why does the narrator desire to return to Mary's, and what stops him? Why do you think he says that he was invisible to Mary?

Epilogue

Summary

The narrator has told his story, and asks us what else he could have done. The narrator says that he has taken some time out, drank liquor, dreamed, and read books. He uses the word "hibernation" to describe his current status.

He still thinks about his grandfather and the deathbed advice, wrestling with what the man meant, and with how to put the advice into practice. The narrator says he is pondering the lessons of his life. He will leave it up to others to decide whether or not he understood history correctly. He wonders about responsibility for history, and about how people can save themselves.

The one specific incident that the narrator talks about is having met Mr. Norton in the subway. Their meeting is brief and, at least for Mr. Norton, disturbing. He does not recognize the narrator, is confused about how the narrator knows his name, and, most of all, has no idea what the narrator means by accusing Mr. Norton of being this man's destiny. Mr. Norton ducks into an available subway car, and the narrator gets a big laugh from it. Then he goes back to his unnoticed home and continues being lost in his thoughts.

Analysis

Like the Prologue, the Epilogue takes place inside the narrator's head. It is his last chance to explain his life and his choices. He gives the impression that he feels he made no choices, because

Epilogue

history put him where he is.

If we were to meet the narrator, or someone like him, on a city street, we would be likely to assume that the person is mentally disturbed. As we have seen, characters in the novel are frequently accused of being "crazy" for what they say, when in fact there may be other explanations for their words.

Mr. Norton is perplexed by being told that he is the narrator's destiny. Of course, the narrator is merely referring to something that Mr. Norton himself had said. Time has passed, but, when we think about it and try to actually figure out time in the novel, we realize that not a great many years have passed since Mr. Norton and the narrator were in the same car on that Southern campus.

Towards the end of the Epilogue, the narrator mentions that he has been writing it all down, which explains the book we have been reading. He goes on to predict that invisibility is universal, and to suggest that, in some way, he is speaking for the reader.

Study Questions

1. To what does the narrator compare reality's irresistibility?
2. To what does the narrator give credit for his invisibility?
3. Regarding his life and his future, what has the narrator often tried to find out?
4. Where does the narrator say that one goes when one steps outside the narrow borders of what men call reality?
5. Whom does the narrator suggest should be asked about this?
6. Towards what does the narrator wonder if he must strive?
7. Why does the narrator feel sure that Mr. Norton will ask him for directions?
8. What street is Mr. Norton trying to find?
9. What answer does the narrator give himself to the question "why do I write?"
10. What possibility about himself does the narrator recognize at the end of the Epilogue?

Answers

1. The narrator compares the irresistibility of reality to a club.

2. The narrator gives credit to his invisibility to his having gone "in everyone's way but [his] own," and of having "also been called one thing and another while no one really wished to hear what [he] called [himself]."

3. Regarding his life and his future, the narrator has often tried to find out what is the next phase for him.

4. The narrator says that when one steps outside the narrow borders of what men call reality, one steps into chaos or imagination.

5. The narrator suggests that one should ask Rinehart about this, since he is the master.

6. The narrator wonders if he must strive towards colorlessness.

7. At first, the narrator feels sure that Mr. Norton will ask him for directions, because the narrator imagines that Mr. Norton might feel embarrassed by not knowing something in front of a fellow white man. Then, the narrator feels sure that Mr. Norton will ask him because it is inevitable.

8. Mr. Norton is trying to find Centre Street.

9. In answer to his question "why do I write," the narrator says that he has learned some things, despite himself.

10. At the end of the Epilogue, the narrator recognizes the possibility that his having overstayed his hibernation was a social crime, and that, perhaps, even an invisible man has a socially responsible role to play.

Suggested Essay Topics

1. Describe the narrator's tone of voice in the Epilogue. He is explaining himself—how does he do that, and what impressions does his mood give you? Be sure to support your points with details from the text.

Epilogue

2. What is your reaction to the narrator's meeting with Mr. Norton? How do they act and react? How is what the narrator says reminiscent of what the Vet has to say while tending Mr. Norton's wounds, in Chapter Three?

SECTION THREE

Sample Analytical Paper Topics

Topic #1

Several times in *Invisible Man*, a character states that another character is crazy. Pick two examples of this, and describe what is happening. What do these moments have in common, and why does one character say that the other is crazy?

Outline

I. Thesis Statement: *In several scenes of* Invisible Man, *a character states that another character is crazy; each character seems to have a specific reason for saying this.*

II. The scene at the narrator's grandfather's deathbed

    A. The dying man is thought to be crazy

    B. The children are rushed away

    C. The narrator hears his grandfather's words

    D. The advice turns out to make a lot of sense

III. "the Vet" tends to Mr. Norton at The Golden Day

    A. Mr. Norton asks about the Vet's history

    B. The Vet comments on Mr. Norton and the narrator

    C. Mr. Norton says the Vet is crazy

    D. The Vet doesn't sound crazy, but is in an insane asylum

Sample Analytical Paper Topics

IV. The narrator says that Ras the Exhorter is crazy
   A. The narrator and Tod Clifton are fighting with Ras
   B. Ras is disappointed with them, and tells them so
   C. He is eloquent, and his words hurt them
   D. The narrator tells Ted Clifton that Ras is crazy

Topic #2

Pick three specific actions by characters other than the narrator. What does each action reveal about the character, and how can we judge these people on the basis of what they do?

Outline

I. Thesis Statement: *The specific actions in* Invisible Man *tell us much about the characters and give us a basis for judging them.*

II. Dr. Bledsoe blames the narrator for what happened to Mr. Norton
   A. Bledsoe protects himself, doesn't take a risk
   B. He is unwilling to oppose the power structure
   C. Shows the narrator that principles are useless
   D. One cannot fight aganist a "machine of people"

III. Lucius Brockway attacks the narrator
   A. Brockway does not wait for the narrator to explain
   B. He is paranoid about losing his job
   C. It does not occur to him that he cannot win the fight
   D. When it is over, he seems pathetic

IV. Sybil asks the narrator to act as though he is raping her
   A. She sees the narrator as "a black buck," not as a person
   B. She wants the narrator to participate in her fantasy
   C. She does not wonder if the idea offends him
   D. She does not consider that he has emotions

Topic #3

The novel describes various aspects of the narrator's life, when he was in different places, doing different things. Which part of his life do you think was the best for him? Why?

Outline

I. Thesis Statement: *This novel describes various aspects of the narrator's life, in some of which the narrator was happier and more fulfilled than in others.*

II. His college years
    A. He remembers those times with loving detail
    B. He remembers his teachers with admiration
    C. He wanted to do a good job of chauffeuring Mr. Norton
    D. He dreaded leaving the college

III. Coming to New York
    A. He was very excited
    B. He found all of the new stimuli fascinating, and tiring
    C. He has dreams about his future
    D. He made at least one friend: Mary

IV. Working for the brotherhood
    A. He believed strongly in the work that he did
    B. The work utilized his public speaking skills
    C. He was encouraged to think of all people as equals
    D. He was given a lot of responsibility

SECTION FOUR

Bibliography

Bishop, John. *Ralph Ellison*. Black Americans of Achievement. Chelsea House Publishers. New York, 1988

Ellison, Ralph. *Invisible Man*. Vintage Books (30th Anniversary Edition.)

Emanuel, James A. and Gross, Theodore L., eds. *Dark Symphony: Negro Literature in America*. The Free Press, Collier-Macmillian, Limited. New York. 1968. pgs. 253-294.

Ousby, Ian. *Fifty American Novels: A Reader's Guide*. Heinemann, London. 1979. pgs. 329–334.

Reilly, John M., ed. *Twentieth Century Interpretations of Invisible Man*. Prentice-Hall, Inc. Englewood Cliffs, New Jersey. 1970.

REA's Test Preps
The Best in Test Preparation

- REA "Test Preps" are far **more** comprehensive than any other test preparation series
- Each book contains up to **eight** full-length practice exams based on the most recent exam
- **Every** type of question likely to be given on the exams is included
- Answers are accompanied by **full** and **detailed** explanations

REA has published over 60 Test Preparation volumes in several series. They include:

Advanced Placement Exams (APs)
Biology
Calculus AB & Calculus BC
Chemistry
Computer Science
English Language & Composition
English Literature & Composition
European History
Government & Politics
Physics
Psychology
Spanish Language
United States History

College Level Examination Program (CLEP)
American History I
Analysis & Interpretation of Literature
College Algebra
Freshman College Composition
General Examinations
Human Growth and Development
Introductory Sociology
Principles of Marketing

SAT II: Subject Tests
American History
Biology
Chemistry
French
German
Literature

SAT II: Subject Tests (continued)
Mathematics Level IC, IIC
Physics
Spanish
Writing

Graduate Record Exams (GREs)
Biology
Chemistry
Computer Science
Economics
Engineering
General
History
Literature in English
Mathematics
Physics
Political Science
Psychology
Sociology

ACT - American College Testing Assessment

ASVAB - Armed Service Vocational Aptitude Battery

CBEST - California Basic Educational Skills Test

CDL - Commercial Driver's License Exam

CLAST - College Level Academic Skills Test

ELM - Entry Level Mathematics

ExCET - Exam for Certification of Educators in Texas

FE (EIT) - Fundamentals of Engineering Exam

FE Review - Fundamentals of Engineering Review

GED - High School Equivalency Diploma Exam (US & Canadian editions)

GMAT - Graduate Management Admission Test

LSAT - Law School Admission Test

MAT - Miller Analogies Test

MCAT - Medical College Admission Test

MSAT - Multiple Subjects Assessment for Teachers

NTE - National Teachers Exam

PPST - Pre-Professional Skills Test

PSAT - Preliminary Scholastic Assessment Test

SAT I - Reasoning Test

SAT I - Quick Study & Review

TASP - Texas Academic Skills Program

TOEFL - Test of English as a Foreign Language

RESEARCH & EDUCATION ASSOCIATION
61 Ethel Road W. • Piscataway, New Jersey 08854
Phone: (908) 819-8880

Please send me more information about your Test Prep Books

Name _____

Address _____

City _____ State _____ Zip _____

The Best Test Preparation for the

LSAT
Law School Admission Test

**COMPLETE COACHING
& REVIEW COURSE plus...
6 FULL-LENGTH EXAMS**
written by <u>test experts</u>

*Completely
Up-to-Date
Based on the
Current Format
of the LSAT*

➤ **LSAT Exercise Drills for all test sections**

➤ **LSAT Study Course Schedule**

PLUS...expert test tips and strategies for answering the different types of questions found on the exam — to help you achieve a **TOP SCORE**

 Research & Education Association

Available at your local bookstore or order directly from us by sending in coupon below.

RESEARCH & EDUCATION ASSOCIATION
61 Ethel Road W., Piscataway, New Jersey 08854
Phone: (908) 819-8880

☐ Payment enclosed
☐ Visa ☐ Master Card

Charge Card Number

Expiration Date: _____ / _____
                   Mo   Yr

Please ship REA's **"LSAT"** @ $19.95 plus $4.00 for shipping.

Name _____

Address _____

City _____ State _____ Zip _____

The Best Test Preparation for the

GRE
GRADUATE RECORD EXAMINATION
GENERAL TEST

6 full-length exams

Completely Up-to-Date Based on the Current Format of the GRE

➤ All of the exam sections prepared by test experts in the particular subject fields

➤ The *ONLY* test preparation book with detailed explanations to every exam question to help you achieve a *TOP SCORE*

➤ Includes in-depth reviews of all test areas with expert test tips and strategies for answering the different types of questions found on the exam

PLUS... a **MATH REVIEW** with drills to build math skills for quantitative sections, and a **VOCABULARY LIST** with word drills of the most frequently tested words on the GRE

REA *Research & Education Association*

Available at your local bookstore or order directly from us by sending in coupon below.

| **RESEARCH & EDUCATION ASSOCIATION** |
| 61 Ethel Road W. • Piscataway, New Jersey 08854 |
| Phone: (908) 819-8880 |

VISA | **MasterCard**

☐ Payment enclosed
☐ Visa ☐ Master Card

Charge Card Number

Expiration Date: ____ / ____
                  Mo   Yr

Please ship **"GRE General Test"** @ $19.95 plus $4.00 for shipping.

Name _____

Address _____

City _____ State _____ Zip _____

Available at your local bookstore or order directly from us by sending in coupon below.

RESEARCH & EDUCATION ASSOCIATION
61 Ethel Road W., Piscataway, New Jersey 08854
Phone: (908) 819-8880

☐ Payment enclosed
☐ Visa ☐ Master Card

Charge Card Number

Expiration Date: _____ / _____
                    Mo   Yr

Please ship **"Handbook of English"** @ $17.95 plus $4.00 for shipping.

Name _____

Address _____

City _____ State _____ Zip _____

REA's **Problem Solvers**

The "PROBLEM SOLVERS" are comprehensive supplemental textbooks designed to save time in finding solutions to problems. Each "PROBLEM SOLVER" is the first of its kind ever produced in its field. It is the product of a massive effort to illustrate almost any imaginable problem in exceptional depth, detail, and clarity. Each problem is worked out in detail with a step-by-step solution, and the problems are arranged in order of complexity from elementary to advanced. Each book is fully indexed for locating problems rapidly.

ACCOUNTING
ADVANCED CALCULUS
ALGEBRA & TRIGONOMETRY
AUTOMATIC CONTROL
 SYSTEMS/ROBOTICS
BIOLOGY
BUSINESS, ACCOUNTING, & FINANCE
CALCULUS
CHEMISTRY
COMPLEX VARIABLES
COMPUTER SCIENCE
DIFFERENTIAL EQUATIONS
ECONOMICS
ELECTRICAL MACHINES
ELECTRIC CIRCUITS
ELECTROMAGNETICS
ELECTRONIC COMMUNICATIONS
ELECTRONICS
FINITE & DISCRETE MATH
FLUID MECHANICS/DYNAMICS
GENETICS
GEOMETRY

HEAT TRANSFER
LINEAR ALGEBRA
MACHINE DESIGN
MATHEMATICS for ENGINEERS
MECHANICS
NUMERICAL ANALYSIS
OPERATIONS RESEARCH
OPTICS
ORGANIC CHEMISTRY
PHYSICAL CHEMISTRY
PHYSICS
PRE-CALCULUS
PROBABILITY
PSYCHOLOGY
STATISTICS
STRENGTH OF MATERIALS &
 MECHANICS OF SOLIDS
TECHNICAL DESIGN GRAPHICS
THERMODYNAMICS
TOPOLOGY
TRANSPORT PHENOMENA
VECTOR ANALYSIS

*If you would like more information about any of these books,
complete the coupon below and return it to us or visit your local bookstore.*

RESEARCH & EDUCATION ASSOCIATION
61 Ethel Road W. • Piscataway, New Jersey 08854
Phone: (908) 819-8880

Please send me more information about your Problem Solver Books

Name _____

Address _____

City _____ State _____ Zip _____

Available at your local bookstore or order directly from us by sending in coupon below.

RESEARCH & EDUCATION ASSOCIATION
61 Ethel Road W., Piscataway, New Jersey 08854
Phone: (908) 819-8880

☐ Payment enclosed
☐ Visa ☐ Master Card

Charge Card Number

Expiration Date: _____ / _____
                     Mo   Yr

Please ship REA's **"SAT II: Literature"** @ $14.95 plus $4.00 for shipping.

Name _____

Address _____

City _____ State _____ Zip _____

THE NEW SAT

The Very Best Coaching & Study Course
Completely Up-To-Date for the *New* SAT

SIX Full-Length Practice Tests with a *Diagnostic Test* to pinpoint your strong and weak areas

- **Test-Taking Strategies** with study schedule and tips that raise students' scores
- **Verbal Skills Review** covering the vocabulary needed for the new SAT; methods for determining definitions of unfamiliar words; the most frequently tested words; drills to sharpen skills
- **Intensive Practice with Explanations** for Sentence Completions, Analogies, and for the new Critical Reading section
- **Math Skills Review** covering Arithmetic, Algebra, Geometry, and Word Problems; practice drills
- **Intensive Math Practice with Explanations** for the Regular (multiple-choice) Math Section, the Quantitative Comparisons, and the new Student-Produced Response section
- **Detailed, easy-to-follow explanations and solutions to every test question**

- Prepared by a team of SAT tutors and test experts thoroughly experienced in the specifics of each particular subject
- Plus...a Guide to Choosing a College, with valuable advice on how to choose and apply to the college of your choice

REA's SAT includes everything you need to score high and build your confidence for the most important test of your academic career

REA *Research & Education Association*

Available at your local bookstore or order directly from us by sending in coupon below.

RESEARCH & EDUCATION ASSOCIATION
61 Ethel Road W., Piscataway, New Jersey 08854
Phone: (908) 819-8880

VISA **MasterCard**

Charge Card Number

☐ Payment enclosed
☐ Visa ☐ Master Card

Expiration Date: _____ / _____
                    Mo   Yr

Please ship REA's **"SAT I"** @ $14.95 plus $4.00 for shipping.

Name _____

Address _____

City _____ State _____ Zip _____